THE ABC OF
Lettering

THE ABC OF

Lettering

J. I. BIEGELEISEN, M.A.

INSTRUCTOR, SCHOOL OF INDUSTRIAL ART, NEW YORK CITY

HARPER & BROTHERS · · NEW YORK AND LONDON

BOOK DESIGN BY THE AUTHOR

AFFECTIONATELY

DEDICATED

TO MY WIFE

Contents

List of Illustrations

Preface

IN PREPARING this book, I have not sought to add just another to the existing collection of lettering books, but rather to present one which would be uniquely valuable. Some books stress lettering for poster artists, others for sign painters, and still others for reproduction letterers. This lettering manual was planned for the practical utility of show-card writers, poster artists, snop apprentices, theatrical and display letterers, reproduction letterers, and commercial art teachers and students. The system of teaching here developed does not aim to shorten the process of learning to letter; its main object is to make the process thorough.

This is a distinctive book in the field of lettering because it can rightfully lay claim to the following outstanding features:

1. ANALYTICAL APPROACH—Because this text was designed for such a varied audience, the material it presents has been meticulously analyzed from many points of view. The apparently simple operation of making a single stroke, for instance, has been described with the exactness of a slow-motion picture camera.

The anatomy of each letter and symbol has been analyzed and reduced to its simplest form by diagrammatic and verbal exposition; and an abundance of full-sized drill charts are included to aid in developing the technique of lettering. In general, instruction has been in keeping with the pedagogic principle of stressing what to *do* and how to do it correctly, rather than what *not* to do.

2. COMPLETENESS—As pointed out, this book is designed both as a text for students and as a manual for professionals. It will be found a handy reference text for all levels of experience, as it deals with the entire range of lettering technique from single-stroke freehand to fine reproduction work.

No expense has been spared to present the work with consummate thoroughness. The alphabets have been divided into upper case, lower case, numerals and signs, and each of these divisions has been placed on an individual page. In no instance is it left to the reader's imagination to supply missing symbols, for he will find the plates complete in every detail.

3. CONSISTENCY—The author, a teacher of lettering, has tried not to lose sight of logical arrangement in organizing the points of learning. Once having established a mode of presentation he has endeavored to adhere to it consistently.

A chapter is devoted to a discussion of the tools and equipment necessary for students and professionals, and each tool is separately discussed. The alphabets are complete and progressively arranged. The classification of material for study and reference is equally consistent. The exercises are in order, and there is one page of text to each alphabet to explain the uses, adaptations, and highlights; and lettering terms are defined and illustrated.

4. PRACTICABILITY—The alphabets included in this repertory have been expressly limited to classic and contemporary styles which are standard, practical, and devoid of cheap mannerisms. Some of them are original designs, while others are adaptations of standard type faces.

It is the opinion of the author and many of his professional colleagues that modern type designs offer an excellent source of inspiration for hand lettering. Goudy, the dean of type designers, in his *Elements of Lettering*, says:

> Lettering based on or suggested by accepted type-forms does not
> deny the artist ample opportunity to shape his letters more freely
> or space them more precisely than fixed and implacable metal types
> allow.

It is imperative to point out that all the alphabets shown in this collection were lettered by hand. The characters were reproduced large enough to make the typical features and singular traits of each alphabet easily discernible.

The author has had a wide commercial experience as a letterer, and is at present teaching this subject at the School of Industrial Art, headed by George K. Gombarts. The craftsmanship displayed in the lettering plates, which some of my students helped to prepare, is evidence of the merits of the teaching technique here outlined.

For spending their summer Sundays in assisting in the compilation of the alphabet charts, I wish at this time to express my sincere gratitude to the following of my students: Bernard Gordon, Julius Levy, Amerigo Manfredi, Joseph Paggioli, Anthony Russo, Charles Scimecca, Leonard Silverman, and Leo Widrowitz.

My heartfelt thanks go to my wife and silent partner, whose assistance throughout the book has been of inestimable value.

To Mr. Arnold Bank and Mr. Simon Shulman, I am grateful for their kindly critical reading of this manuscript.

Special thanks go to M. Grumbacher Company and to the Hunt Pen Company for their permission to use the plates demonstrating the brush and pen series, respectively.

J. I. BIEGELEISEN

New York City
February, 1940

THE ABC OF
Lettering

Introduction

MANY an ambitious young man with a flair for art cherishes a yearning for a career as a commercial artist. He feels that in this profession he would best express himself artistically, and at the same time be amply recompensed for his efforts.

Numerous schools offer courses in "commercial art" designed to satisfy this artistic yearning. A boy registering in one of these courses, however, will soon find himself lost in the ramifications of this vast subject. Indeed, the subject of commercial art is so vast, that it readily becomes vague.

PHASES OF COMMERCIAL ART—Commercial art does not exist as an entity. It is a group term for all ramifications such as lettering, costume designing, container designing, poster work, fashion drawing, book illustrating, etc. And the divisions of commercial art do not end here. They are subdivided into men's fashions, women's fashions, book-jacket designing, and still-life representation, etc. The fields of specialization continue even further. Certain commercial artists are renowned for their expert rendering of men's hats, or women's shoes, or lovely lips; others have attained fame for child figures, animals, or gnomes. In each case, the artist has become outstanding in one specialized phase of art, and his work, wherever viewed, can readily be identified.

LETTERING AS AN ART—Commercial art, we may then say, is the name given to the entire field of industrial art and design. A student registering for a commercial art course should realize that he cannot possibly become master of this entire field. Such an accomplishment would be possible only if everyone were as gifted as Leonardo da Vinci, who excelled in many arts, including lettering. The common mortal must remember that art is long, but life is short.

Many modern illustrators cannot do their own lettering. The freedom to which they have become accustomed in drawing is not compatible with the precise technique of lettering, and they are unable to control the lettering brush with the necessary precision. This fact does not affect their success as illustrators. It merely shows that lettering is an art in itself. In this era of specialization a student must carefully evaluate his talents and inclinations and then make his choice. This book is for those who have chosen the art of lettering.

SPECIALIZATION IN LETTERING—The question may be raised whether, in this ever-changing world of ours, it is not rather risky to specialize in this one field—whether the hand letterer's art might not someday be replaced by a mechanical device.

There is some basis for such speculation when one reflects that the field for the commercial artist whose art consists solely of copying (be it a skyscraper or a frankfurter) has narrowed down appreciably in the past ten or fifteen years. What with the advent and perfection of color photography, it is only natural that the "specialist" who can draw a pretty picture from life or memory should be suffering from diminishing returns—financially speaking. But this condition is not and never will be true of those occupations, like lettering, in which the imagination and creative sense are brought into play.

Indeed, years ago a good artist was one who could faithfully portray a subject "as if it were alive." Today, photography can accomplish this feat with far greater fidelity, and in infinitely less time.

In choosing a phase for specialization in commercial art which will reasonably withstand the element of "changing times" consider this criterion: Is it an art based on creative or on realistic representation? Lettering offers a splendid opportunity as a creative phase of commercial art, and mechanical ingenuity will never replace the professional hand lettering artist. For just as there can never be a machine to compose a sonnet or a symphony, there can never be a device to do creative lettering or to design a layout.

TYPE COMPARED WITH HAND LETTERING—At this point it may seem that the possibility of type as a rival to hand lettering has not been thought of. On the contrary, the question has been well considered, and the general conclusion has been that there is no conflict between these two graphic media; there is a definite field for each.

Type should not loom in the minds of letterers as a devilish device which competes with their art. Type, originated as hand-drawn design, should be thought of as lettering frozen in its best form. The knowledge of lettering should, therefore, not be limited to the hand letterer. It is equally important for the typographer. Stern, a recognized printing authority, in his *Introduction to Typography*, says: "To be able to letter well is one of the greatest assets a typographer can possess."

Whereas the unvarying calculated exactness of type is a decided advantage in many instances, the individualized and flexible use of hand lettering adds distinction to modern commercial art work. Hand lettering, which is "custom-made," is not subject to the rigidity that governs type, and it can be adjusted to suit any situation and to express distinctive qualities. This is not feasible with type, which comes "ready-made."

ADVANTAGES OF LETTERING—In the case of individual show-card and poster work, hand lettering is not only more personal than type, it is also more economical. An experienced letterer can with a minimum of effort letter in many cards a day, each with the particular color and lettering style best suited to the subject. He "writes with his brush," as it were, and dispenses with the trouble of setting up type and making plates. On the other hand, wherever type would be more effective or more economical, it should be used freely.

IMPORTANCE OF LETTERING—The importance of lettering and the study of lettering cannot be overemphasized. It is enough to point out that, whereas excellent posters are

4

made without benefit of illustration, posters without lettering of some kind would be a rare sight. Austin Cooper, in his *Making a Poster*, says: "I think we may safely say that of all single factors in the poster's composition, *lettering* is the most important."

DIVISIONS OF LETTERING—Lettering in itself is a rather broad field. It may be classified according to its *use* as (1) sign painting, (2) poster lettering, and (3) reproduction lettering; or according to the *tool* as (1) brush lettering, (2) pen lettering, and (3) mechanical-instrument lettering.

CHARACTERISTICS OF LETTERING—Lettering is a precise art. The letterer, unlike the illustrator or still-life painter, is faced with the fact that each stroke in forming a letter is vital, not merely a matter of momentary discrimination. Lettering can be judged objectively and any inaccuracies in letter forms easily detected. It is not to be inferred that the accuracy and precision of lettering inhibit artistic expression, for experienced lettering artists can give full play to their creative faculties.

STANDARD LETTERING—Although lettering has been characterized as a precise art, it is not one which involves soulless mechanical perfection. The art of lettering allows for many improvisations, but it is foolhardy for the beginner to attempt to create new lettering styles before he has mastered the old "safe" ones. Before he dares defy convention he should have an appreciation of basic design and standard letter forms. The beginner is often tempted to camouflage his lack of professional finish behind a convenient cloak of alleged creativeness.

In order to be prepared to do original work, a student should first have a thorough groundwork in fundamentals. Originality should come only as the outgrowth of past experience. This applies to the art of lettering as to other arts. Frederic Goudy puts it this way: "Eccentricity of form becomes unpardonable affectation when attempted by the untrained amateur."

The beginner in lettering is, therefore, urged to adhere to rigid standards, to strive for accuracy and character, and to conform to accepted alphabets. When he has lost his hand-heaviness, has perfected his strokes, and has developed appreciation and skill in basic letter forms, he may then enter the realm of creative work. Impromptu letter inventions should be kept strictly within the province of men of training, experience, and imagination.

LETTERING AS DESIGN—Although the letters of the alphabet are usually thought of as symbols of recorded language, they may also be considered from the point of view of pure intrinsic design. To those with a keen sense and appreciation of design, the letter form is a thing of beauty even though it be a symbol of a language they cannot fathom. Characters of the Arabic, Hebrew, and Greek alphabets, for example, provide a splendid study of calligraphic beauty. For purposes of design appreciation, it matters little whether or not we have a literal understanding of the strange symbols.

LEGIBILITY IN LETTERING—Care must be taken not to allow thoughts of mass, proportion, and weight to overshadow the letterer's obligation to the public. He must remember that readability is the prime requisite of the written word. The lettering artist should never lose sight of the fact that the symbols he employs are tools for conveying an intelligible message. The less the identity of a letter is obscured—that is, the more *legible* it is—the *better* it is and the closer it comes to fulfilling its true function. Through extensive reading even the layman has a mental picture of the letters of the alphabet. The closer the letterer's art approaches that common concept the more legible the letter is said to be.

Some authorities feel that the lower-case is generally more legible than the upper-case because in printed books and in natural handwriting greater use is made of small, or lower-case, letters than of capitals. On the other hand, it is readily seen that public signs, warning signals, street name plates, exit signs, railroad and road signs, and all important notices are printed entirely in capital letters to convey a message quickly. It seems to the author that the eye follows capital letters with less tedium than it does lower-case letters. Capitals can be read in a straight line without having to detour for the ascenders and descenders of lower-case letters. However, the comparative legibility of the upper- and lower-case alphabets is a question open for discussion. What is your thought on the subject?

LETTERER'S REPERTORY—The student of lettering need not burden himself with an overloaded repertory of alphabets. After mastering brush manipulation he should learn a few practical styles so well that he will have them at his finger tips ready for use at all times. Even a professional letterer does not employ numberless alphabets; he usually has a few "favorites" which he finds most practical for his work.

It is better to learn several standard alphabets thoroughly than to have a superficial knowledge of many "stunt" styles.

DEVELOPMENT OF A GOOD LETTERER—If you have chosen lettering as a career, remember that it takes years of experience to master the art. The beginner will at first find his hand heavy and trembling. The knowledge that each stroke has a definite meaning creates a tension which only experience can relieve. Instruction, persistent practice, and self-discipline will provide this necessary experience. Lettering, like the mastery of a musical instrument, calls for hours of practice each day, until such time when there is perfect coordination of hand and mind. Only then will the letterer have attained a level of craftsmanship.

LETTERING AS A VOCATION—A good letterer holds within his grasp the basic knowledge for related lucrative vocations. The determination to become a *letterer* is not specific enough, since there is a wide range of positions in the field of lettering. There are specialists who do outdoor scaffold bulletin work of such large dimensions that the artist by comparison appears to be about the size of the dot over the "i." Then there are those who specialize in fine reproduction work as detailed as a delicate engraving. Between these two extremes, lettering offers many other vocational opportunities. Your special niche in lettering will depend on your inclination, your ability, and the pressure of circumstances.

Hand lettering is the basic art for sign painting and show-card writing. The field for show-card writers is at present more extensive than that for sign painters. A permanent sign, representing a somewhat large monetary investment, is used for a long time before the sign painter is called in to replace it. Show-cards, however, are of a temporary nature and used in quantity in every business; and since they cost less they are changed regularly. You surely have seen cards of one kind or another in the drug, clothing, dry goods, jewelry, millinery, shoe, hardware, radio, stationery, candy, book, dress, cleaning, flower, furniture, art supply, paint or department store in your neighborhood. The beginner in lettering will usually find it possible to obtain his initial experience in the professional field by gaining a foothold in show-card writing.

WHAT A LETTERER CAN DO—Besides working on show-cards a letterer can specialize in designing and lettering price tags, movie titles, store displays, theater lobby fronts, seals, letterheads, trade marks, book jackets, magazine headings and story titles, greeting cards, brochures, magazine and newspaper advertisements, etc.

WHERE A LETTERER CAN WORK—In general, good letterers are in demand at sign and show-card shops, lithography houses, silk screen shops, window display studios, advertising agencies, publishing houses, and the art departments of newspapers and large chain and department stores.

Also, there are opportunities for work in conjunction with expert illustrators whose lettering is not up to par for professional work.

LETTERING APPRENTICE—A student of lettering should constantly be on the alert for lettering displayed in stores, magazines, and exhibitions. If he is fortunate enough to serve his apprenticeship in a studio-shop, he should not think it below his dignity to do odd jobs such as filling in, erasing, mixing color, washing brushes, etc. He should respect the experience of his superiors and welcome every opportunity to observe the master craftsman at work. As Robert Browning said in his "Rabbi Ben Ezra":

> Here, work enough to watch
>
> The Master work, and catch
>
> Hints of the proper craft, tricks of the tool's true play.

QUALIFICATIONS OF A GOOD LETTERER—The field of lettering is open to both men and women. Naturally, those with the higher qualifications and an inherent liking for the execution of letter forms will meet with earlier and steadier success.

In addition to the ability to do good lettering, a letterer should have a fair background in art. He should have a feeling for design, color harmony, and rhythm. He should understand the importance of mass, shape, and balance. He should be familiar with layout and copy writing, and be able to combine this knowledge with the rules for correct spacing and grouping of words and ideas.

Besides these prerequisites, a fair general education will stand him in good stead. No employer or client will long tolerate bad spelling, poor trade mathematics, and ill-breeding. In addition, a pleasant speaking voice, a sense of fair play to clients, employer, and fellow employees, good trade judgment, and personal neatness are assets in getting and holding any position.

If you possess these attributes, if you letter well and with reasonable speed, there is a happy professional future in store for you.

Equipment

CHAPTER 2

THIS chapter deals with the full array of materials that are the stock in trade of both the student letterer and the professional. Do not despair if you cannot immediately have everything. Success in learning lettering does not depend solely upon an elaborate assortment of tools and iigs. It depends rather upon your aptitudes, your ambitions, your effort, and the wise purchase and use of a few good tools.

The serious student is urged not to equip himself with a sensational "amateur outfit." Such paraphernalia may be all right for those who wish to take up lettering as a hobby. But for professional use this means a constant struggle with inferior equipment. It is better to purchase professional tools as you require them, and build up a complete set of equipment as you gain in experience. For beginner's practice work, the fundamental implements are some pencils, a few show-card brushes, some paint or ink, a ruler, and a T square. You don't have to buy any special paper; use ordinary newspapers, using the columns as guide lines.

The materials for lettering may be classified as (1) tools, (2) mediums, (3) surfaces, (4) equipment, and (5) working auxiliaries.

TOOLS

Pencils—Pencils are used for ruling guide lines, for laying out the copy, for tracing, etc. They come in various grades, from very soft to very hard (ranging from 6B to 9H). A medium-soft black pencil (HB) is best for general work and studio use.

Charcoal or Chalk—Whether you do freehand or reproduction lettering, you can use charcoal or chalk for making guide lines and laying out the lettering. For work on a dark surface, where charcoal would not be visible, chalk is better. To avoid soiling your hands during handling, it is wise to buy charcoal and chalk in pencil rather than stick form.

Pens—For pen lettering you may have your choice of ball-bearing pens, Esterbrook drawlet pens, pointed drawing pens, shading nibs, etc. The most popular are the Speedball pens. These come in different numbered sizes and produce strokes from as fine as a hairline to about ¼ inch or more in thickness. Most lettering pens are manufactured in various nibs to produce square, oblong, round, or oval strokes. An art supply dealer, when informed of the use to which you mean to put the pen, can aid you in your selection. For Speedball pens and their accompanying strokes, see Figure E, page 15.

Brushes—Lettering brushes are of three types: flat show-card, round show-card, and rigger. The flat brush is good for large, one-stroke work, while the round brush is adaptable to both built-up and single-stroke letters. Rigger brushes are reserved for script

HANDLE

FERRULE

HEEL

HAIR

CHISEL

lettering, fine reproduction work, outlining, and scrolls.

Buy the best lettering brush obtainable. You will find it smart economy of time, money, and patience to use a brush as good as, or even better than, that of a professional letterer, whose skill can to some extent help him overcome the stubborn resistance of an inferior brush.

Round show-card brushes come in graduated sizes ranging from No. 1 through No. 20, see Figure A, page 15. The No. 8 with medium-length bristles is the best investment for the beginner who can afford but one brush, because it produces a stroke of intermediate thickness. It may be interesting to note here that the brush exercises shown on pages 41 to 50, were done with just such a brush.

Rulers—Rulers are obtainable in wood, celluloid, or metal, in lengths from 6 to 36 inches. A wooden ruler, good for general measuring, does not always produce a true line, as it is subject to nicks and warping. This defect is only somewhat obviated by a wooden ruler with a metal edge. Celluloid rulers are slightly better, but they too become warped and somewhat nicked.

The steel ruler is the most expensive, and as is so often the case with expensive tools, it is also the most accurate and durable.

Triangles—Another useful tool for general studio work is the triangle. The

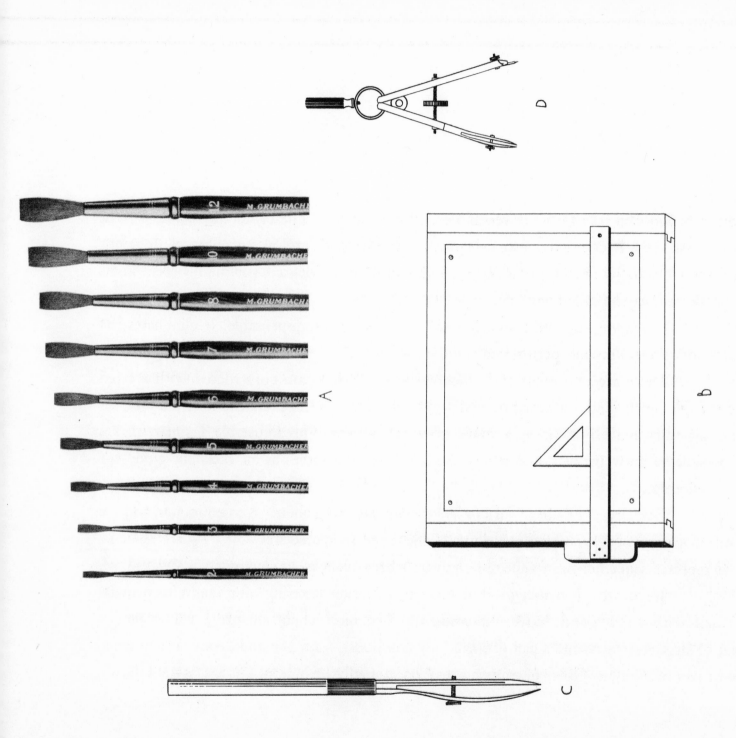

A

B

C

D

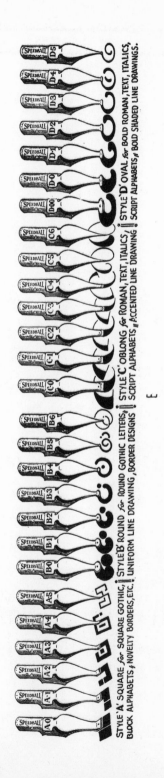

E

STYLE 'A' SQUARE *for* SQUARE GOTHIC, || STYLE 'B' ROUND *for* ROUND GOTHIC LETTERS, || STYLE 'C' OBLONG *for* ROMAN, TEXT, ITALICS, || STYLE 'D' OVAL *for* BOLD ROMAN, TEXT, ITALICS,
BLOCK ALPHABETS, NOVELTY BORDERS, ETC. || UNIFORM LINE DRAWING, BORDER DESIGNS || ACCENTED LINE DRAWING || SCRIPT ALPHABETS || BOLD SHADED LINE DRAWINGS.
SCRIPT ALPHABETS

Essential Lettering Materials

15

opaque or wooden triangle is not recommended for letterers. The celluloid triangle is most commonly used. It comes in various degrees of transparency and in various sizes. It might be a good idea to get one of 30-60 degrees and another of 45 degrees for the different kinds of work you may be called on to do.

T Squares—For professional work a T square is indispensable. It eliminates the guesswork from drawing perpendicular or square lines.

There are two kinds of T squares. Most of them are constructed with a fixed right-angle head rigidly attached to a perpendicular blade. On others the head may be set to an arbitrary angle by means of a thumbscrew attachment. This adjustable T square makes it possible to draw parallel lines at any desired angle and serves as an excellent guide for italic lettering.

T squares are made in various lengths ranging from about 18 to 48 inches, and are made of plain wood, wood with a celluloid edge, or of tempered steel. A T square made of steel represents an efficient lifetime tool; it never warps or nicks; its squareness is always true.

Mechanical Instruments—For fine reproduction lettering, one ought to provide himself with a few good drafting instruments. The most important are a ruling pen, a pair of large compasses and a pair of small bow compasses, with pen and pencil attachments, and a pair of dividers. Other instruments may occasionally be helpful but are not absolutely essential for the lettering artist.

Paper—There is a variety of surfaces suitable for lettering work. Of these, paper is certainly most practical for the beginner. Paper is available in an assortment of colors, sizes, finishes, and thicknesses. The list includes newsprint paper, sign paper, bond paper, ledger paper, etc., and these are sold in sheets, pads, or rolls.

For the practice of lettering with a brush, it is suggested that you buy a 14″ x 22″ newsprint paper pad. This is inexpensive and practical, since the absorbent property of the paper makes it ideal for brushwork. What is more, the pages of a newsprint paper pad do not fall out of the binding as they are turned. Not only is this a feature of economy, but, if each page is dated and numbered, the pad is converted into a one-volume diary of the student's lettering progress.

Show-Card Board—Show-card board, which comes in sizes 22″ x 28″, 28″ x 44″ and 40″ x 60″, is used for poster and display work. This board is available in almost any color, including gold, silver, and brilliant metal foil. It comes in two standard thicknesses: single or double thick.

Illustration and Bristol Board—Illustration board offers a particularly good surface for brush lettering and, since it is white, affords a pleasing contrast with most colors used. Illustration board comes in a slightly pebbled, or "toothed," finish for brushwork, as well as in a kid, or smooth, finish for reproduction lettering work done with a ruling pen.

Bristol board, considerably thinner, offers the same working properties and, regardless of how thin the sheet may be, will not buckle as ordinary paper does when poster color or ink is applied to it.

Beaver Board—Beaver board is the most substantial display material and its special thickness minimizes warping. Another of its advantages lies in the fact that it is available for extra-large jobs, since it comes in jumbo sizes of 4' x 6', 4' x 8', 4' x 10', and 4' x 12'. Recently, coated beaver board has been offered to display men in a limited number of beautiful colors.

MEDIUMS

Show-Card or Poster Colors—Poster, show-card, or tempera colors are different names applied to opaque water colors. They are to be had in jars and tubes in practically every color of the spectrum.

Beginners will find it desirable to use black for their practice work, because it contrasts best with a light paper background. Black is also the ideal color for reproduction lettering, as it photographs exceptionally well.

India Inks—India ink, formerly available only in black, is now manufactured in an assortment of colors, but the black, which is opaque, is most popular for reproduction lettering work. Black India ink when used as a background will not "bleed" through; that is, it will not change the color value of a light poster color applied over it. India ink is better used with a pen than with a brush; it is waterproof; and it dries with a pleasing silky-satin finish.

Letterine—For lettering work where you prefer a high-gloss finish it is best to use letterine. This black composition ink may be applied with brush or pen. It dries with a high lustre, and gives a slightly embossed effect.

EQUIPMENT

Drawing Board—Inferior drawing boards, such as those made of composition board, are not recommended; they do not always line up accurately with the T square and thumbtacks cannot easily be inserted into their hard surfaces.

Good drawing boards are made of basswood and come in sizes from 12″ x 17″ to about 31″ x 42″.

Drawing Table—The ideal drawing table is so constructed that you can adjust its height and angle to accommodate any convenient working position. If you cannot afford a table, and you have a knack for simple carpentry, you can hinge a board onto a wall at any level and so adjust it that it can be set at any angle when in use and will hang flat against the wall and out of the way when not in use.

WORKING AUXILIARIES

Sandpaper Block—For keeping a fine point on your lead pencil you will need a sandpaper block. There are also metal blocks, more or less like files, which are of lifelong permanence and are financially within the reach of all.

Sharpener—There are several good means of sharpening pencils. The mechanical rotary sharpener and the electric rotary sharpener produce even-coned points. As a beginner you can manage without either of these if you carry a small 5- or 10-cent sharpener in your pocket. In case you do not own one of these, or if an exceptionally long point is desired, you can use your penknife or a single-edged razor blade.

Palette—Any nonabsorbent surface, such as a glass, mirror, tile, or porcelain dish will serve for relieving the brush of excess paint. A small individual butter plate is perhaps the best of these, because its slightly raised rim keeps the accumulated paint from spreading.

Scotch Tape—Scotch tape, also known as masking tape, is the equivalent of ever-wet gum paper. It is applied without moistening of any kind, and can be removed without marring the surface upon which it has been used. And the same piece of Scotch tape can be used more than once. It is more practical than thumbtacks for fixing a sheet of paper into position, as it obviates the puncturing of holes in paper or drawing board. Scotch tape permits the free sliding of T square and triangle over the drawing surface without interference from protruding thumbtack heads.

Thumbtacks—Keep a supply of thumbtacks handy for heavy-duty fastening work where Scotch tape would not be practical. Tacks come in various sizes and colors.

Rubber Cement—Rubber cement is a handy adhesive. It is easy to use because you do not have to wait for it to dry. Rubber cement, unlike glue, leaves no stain or mark after you rub it off and does not curl or warp even the thinnest paper.

Chamois, Dusters, Rags—These plebeian articles are well known, and in the service of a busy letterer they also become well worn.

Chamois is excellent for erasing charcoal or chalk lines. Dusters are used for removing the residue from art gum; rags for general work and for cleaning brushes and pens.

Knives—For cutting cardboard or beaver board, without a cutting machine, an inexpensive mat knife will do quite well. Such a knife may be bought at a hardware or art supply store. Its blades may be resharpened on a hone or replaced by new ones as the occasion arises.

A small utility or office knife is useful for cutting friskets and thin paper, and for other light work.

Colored Pencils—Assorted colored pencils, as well as crayons, are necessary for "visuals" and other coloring work incidental to sketches and layouts. The pencils are easier to sharpen than the crayons; they do not have the tendency to break so readily; and they are not so much affected by changes in temperature as some of the cheaper crayons.

Erasers—Art gum is familiar to most of you as soap eraser. This is a soft eraser which does not bite into the surface over which it is rubbed. To eliminate the small pieces that fall off during erasing, and also to avoid smudging (especially when erasing on tracing paper), use a kneaded eraser. A new kind of rubber eraser, in the shape of a pencil, is now on the market, and will be found helpful in erasing narrow portions of detailed work.

Smocks and Aprons—Wearing a smock or apron will provide protection against soiling more expensive clothing. At the same time it will provide several well-placed pockets for brushes, pencils, etc.

Lights—Whenever possible, take advantage of natural daylight to do close lettering work. If you find it necessary to work after the sun has set, use a blue "daylight bulb" which simulates natural light to some degree. This will not hurt your eyes so much as the yellow glare of an ordinary bulb, and from a technical point of view it is good because it does not distort color values.

To prevent overhead lights from creating disturbing shadows on the working surface, see that the source of light is over your left shoulder.

A gooseneck lamp, whose flexibility permits adjustment to any convenient angle, will be found particularly handy; it doesn't take up much room on the drawing table and can easily be regulated.

Patented Aids—Do not rely on jigs, patented lettering forms, French curves, and miraculous short cuts for lettering. These devices inhibit freedom of movement, tend to stifle the letterer, and rob the lettering of its vitality. Patented tools are not so dangerous in the hands of an expert, who can use them with discretion, but to the beginner they give a false sense of confidence, and in time become a necessary crutch.

Airbrush—The use of the airbrush or aerograph has been revived, and is no longer used as a sign painter's trick to cover up deficiencies and errors. It is used now for shading and blending effects, as well as for smoothly covering background surfaces.

Card-Cutting Machine—This "guillotine" consists of a long-bladed knife hinged onto a ruled board. These cutting machines come in lengths to accommodate the cutting of different sizes of paper and cardboard. The blade, if used for nothing tougher than cardboard, rarely requires resharpening.

Cut Awl—A cut awl is a portable electric cutting machine for cutting stock into any shape. It can cut display material, such as paper, cardboard, or wood, up to ¾-inch thickness, and is used chiefly to produce cutout lettering and panels for display work.

REFERENCE MATERIAL

Morgue—The strange term "morgue" comes from newspaper slang and refers to the file of miscellaneous clippings collected for future reference. To keep abreast of changing styles and current innovations, and to gain inspiration from the achievements of others in your field, you should maintain an up-to-date morgue. This should include clippings from magazines, industrial catalogues, booklets on stocks and supplies, many alphabet charts, and tidbits about letterers and lettering.

Lettering Terminology

CHAPTER 3

FAMILIES OF ALPHABETS

The four main alphabet families may be classified as:

1. *Gothic or Block*—An alphabet whose elementary parts are composed of even-width strokes; it is a one-thickness letter. See page 139.

2. *Roman*—An alphabet whose elementary parts are composed of fine and accented strokes; it is a thick-and-thin letter. See page 135.

3. *Italic and Script*—Italic, an alphabet whose letters are slanted and unconnected. If connected or joined, it is called Script. See pages 175 and 181.

4. *Text*—A calligraphic alphabet whose elementary parts are composed of strokes of various widths. It retains a pen-drawn quality, and is ornate. Text alphabets include Old English and Diploma. See pages 147 and 151.

CLASSIFICATION OF LETTER FORM

The letter form may be classified under the following categories:

1. Face

   (a) *Light*—A letter whose general slender appearance is unimposing in weight. It gives a gray tone to a mass of copy. See page 167.

   (b) *Dark or Black*—A bold version of a letter, which gives a heavy-set tone to a mass of copy. See page 127.

2. Stroke

    (*a*) *Single-stroke or one-stroke*—A letter whose integral parts or elements are executed with one stroke of the lettering tool. See page 99.

    (*b*) *Built-up*—A letter whose integral parts or elements require more than one stroke of the lettering tool. See page 143.

3. Width

    (*a*) *Condensed*—Lettering that is narrow; and taller than it is wide. See page 111.

    (*b*) *Extended*—Lettering that is wide and spread out; giving a squatty impression. See page 115.

4. Finish

    (*a*) *Serif*—A letter whose terminals are finished off with a shoulder or spur. See page 131.

    (*b*) *Serifless or Sans-serif*—A letter whose terminals are either straight or round, without any extending spur. See page 163.

5. Practicability

    (*a*) *For Text Use*—A simple letter used for main text or reading matter. Legibility is its main characteristic. See page 135.

(*b*) *For Display Use*—An ornate letter used for titles, "spots," displays, and dressy captions. Decoration and design are its predominant features. See pages 159 and 189.

STRUCTURAL PARTS OF LETTER FORM

It might be well at this time to list and define the terminology generally used to denote the structural parts of the letter form:

Upper Case—Uncial, or majuscule, letters, commonly known as capital letters. So called because in printing, these characters are kept in the upper cases or trays of standard type cabinets.

Lower Case—Half-uncial, or minuscule, letters, commonly known as small letters. So called because in printing, these characters are kept in the lower cases or trays of standard type cabinets.

Face—The surface of the letter stroke itself.

Strokes or Elements—The individual structural parts which form a letter.

Stem—The main upright stroke of a letter.

Hairline—The thin, unaccented line of a thick-and-thin letter.

Descender—The element of a lower-case letter which descends below the base line to the drop, or descender, line.

Ascender—The element of a lower-case letter which extends above the main body of the letter, from the waist line to the cap, or ascender, line.

Crossbar—The horizontal stroke across or projecting from the body of a letter.

Serif—The short finishing touch or projecting spur at the beginning or end of a stroke.

Fillet—The connecting bracket blending the serif into the stem.

Curve—The round part of a letter.

Nick—The triangular area formed near the guide line where two strokes meet and blend.

Kern—The curved terminus or ball of an ascender or descender.

Loop or Lobe—The round-bellied element of a letter.

Swash—The free, flourishing taillike element of a letter, as in the Q and R.

Counter—The blank area formed within the lobe of a letter.

The various guide lines used in lettering may be classified as:

Cap, or Ascender, Line—The guide line governing the height of capital letters and ascenders.

"t" Line—The guide line governing the height of the lower-case "t."

Waist Line—The guide line governing the height of the main body of lower-case letters.

Base Line—The guide line determining the base for all capitals, and for the bodies of lower-case letters.

Drop, or Descender, Line—The guide line governing the length of the descenders of lower-case letters.

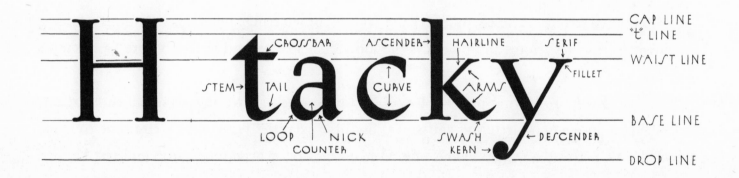

Lettering Exercises

LEARNING to letter is more or less comparable to the mastery of a musical instrument. When learning to play an instrument, such as a piano, you know how essential it is to develop facility in running the fingers over the keyboard—to learn the notes before playing any melodies. And so in lettering—all lettering shapes can be reduced to a number of directional strokes. These strokes are the "notes" of lettering, and a conscientious lettering student learns these notes and practices the individual strokes and letters before he attempts to produce a poster.

In the following pages you will find the notes of lettering arranged in exercises. To develop into a good lettering craftsman, do these exercises faithfully. Determine to make each stroke better than the previous one. When you tire, it is better to stop and rest than to sacrifice the precision of your work by continuing at a low efficiency.

PROCEDURE FOR PRACTICE

Preparation of Paper—Fasten a piece of drawing paper, cardboard, or newsprint paper horizontally onto your drawing board, so that the lower edge of your paper is parallel to, or flush with, the lower edge of the drawing board. See page 15. Using the width of the blade of your T square as a unit of measure, rule your paper into horizontal columns, allowing

31

about ½-inch space between columns.

Or, if it will satisfy your prudent spirit to find some use for yesterday's newspaper, you may use that for practice work. See page 31. Hold the newspaper so that the columns are horizontal, and use the thin lines separating the columns as guide lines.

Preparation of Color—Now for your poster color. Black is best for practice because it contrasts so well with white paper and makes every stroke visible and clear. If you see each stroke well, you cannot fool yourself into believing that a stroke is better than it really is.

Poster color must be of proper consistency. If it is too thick, it will produce a ragged, "dry" stroke. If it has been made watery, the hair of the brush will become wobbly and the color will spread. Should you find that your paint is too thick, add a little water to the jar, and stir the entire contents thoroughly with a stick or old spoon. Do not merely thin the surface, or you will be kept constantly busy adding water to the thick paint.

It isn't quite such an easy job to thicken color if it has accidentally been made too thin. Leave the jar open overnight so that some of the water may evaporate. For a quicker remedy, spread a little of the color on an absorbent piece of cardboard and allow the water to sink into the card. When the excess water has been thus evaporated and drained, use the card as a palette and source of color supply.

Proper Posture—Now a word about the best posture for lettering. For doing close or small work, it is better to be seated. For large work, a standing position will allow far more elbow room.

Hold yourself erect, with both feet flat on the floor. The perfect contact with terra firma will give you the stability and bodily equilibrium necessary for good lettering. Rest the weight of the upper part of your body on your free hand. The hand that guides the brush should never be burdened with the support of the body. To increase freedom of movement even further, remove any long-sleeved garment that you may be wearing—especially if it is one with interfering buttons.

Position of Paper and Paints—To conserve your eyesight and take in a broader view of the job laid out before you, do not bend down too near to your work. See that the paper is in front of you, and a little to the right. Do not tilt the paper at a rakish angle as that will throw your work into confusing perspective.

Adjust your body so that the left hand rests on the drawing board, leaving plenty of room for right-arm movement. For right-handed letterers, paints, inks, water, etc., should be kept at the right side of the drawing table where they will be within easy reach. It would be as wasteful a motion to keep them at the left as it would be to use the right hand and reach around the back of your neck to scratch the left ear.

Holding the Brush—The exact finger position for holding the brush is a controversial question based on individually established working habits. There are three generally accepted positions:

1. *Two-finger hold*, the brush being held between thumb and index finger.

   This is a light hold, and many letterers feel that it affords best control of the brush.

2. *Two-finger hold*, the brush being held between thumb and middle finger.

   The brush is held lightly between the fingers. With the aid of the thumb, the brush is rotated along the side of the middle finger, which serves as a rail. The index finger is slightly extended and does not aid in controlling the brush.

3. *Three-finger hold*, the brush being held by the thumb firmly against the middle finger and controlled by the index finger. This position is similar to that of holding a pencil. It is the favorite of many letterers.

It makes little real difference which hold you favor. The following points are valid for any position:

1. Hold the brush on the ferrule, close down to the heel, but not touching the hair. This permits better control and more speed.

2. Rest the weight of the hand holding the brush on the first knuckle of the "pinky" finger. This reduces friction to a minimum as the hand moves over the paper.

3. Hold the brush in an almost vertical position, with the handle slightly inclined toward you.

4. Hold and manipulate the brush without the direct aid or support of the other hand.

Using the Brush—Your brush will respond to the slightest pressure of the hand. Learn how it behaves so that you may guide it well. Here are a few points to remember about the use of the brush:

1. Remember that the width of a stroke depends upon

   (*a*) The size of the brush

   The larger the brush the wider the natural stroke it will produce.

   (*b*) The amount of pressure applied

   The same brush will produce heavier strokes with greater pressure.

   (*c*) The amount of color used

   A flooded brush will produce a fuller, broader stroke than a drained one.

   (*d*) The position of the brush

   For a single-thick, single-stroke letter, work with the full width of the brush. For round parts of such letters, rotate the brush handle between the fingers as a curve is made.

   For a thick-and-thin, single-stroke letter, work with the width of the brush for the "swell" and with the side of the brush for the "hairline." For round parts of such letters, do *not* rotate the brush handle between the fingers as a curve is made.

2. Keep the brush well charged with color to avoid refilling in the middle of a stroke. A well-charged brush will produce a sharp, smooth, continuous stroke.

3. Smooth or work the charged brush on a palette before applying it to the lettering surface. This removes excess paint, strokes the hair in the proper direction, and produces a cleaner working edge on the brush.

4. Move the entire arm, not just the fingers or the wrist. The larger the lettering the more marked the movement of the arm should be.

5. Point the handle of the brush in the direction of the stroke. For example, when making a capital H, the brush handle *points* toward you as the stroke *moves* toward you. For the horizontal crossbar, the brush handle points toward the right as the brush moves from left to right.

6. Move the brush across the surface vigorously. Timidity and hesitation will bring about undesirable tension and weight. A stroke should be pulled rapidly, for it is as difficult to produce a firm stroke slowly as it is to control a bicycle while riding at a snail's pace.

Stroke Steps—Making a single brush stroke as in Exercise 1, simple and innocent as it appears, may be broken up into five distinct and rhythmic steps. For classroom work, it is best to do this drill in unison, with the instructor tapping out each command, holding it for the number of beats indicated, and gradually increasing the tempo. This drill procedure applies as well to an individual engaged in self-instruction. For both individual and mass instruction it is excellent drill work, and will develop manual discipline, precision, and rhythm. In the personal teaching experience of the author, this system has brought gratifying results.

It should be pointed out that the following drill may be used for all the accompanying exercises, except those on pages 48 and 49.

The five steps in making a simple vertical stroke are:

1. *Touch*   (1 beat)

   The brush, charged with color and smoothed on the palette, is applied to the upper guide line.

2. *Hold*   (2 beats)

   The brush is seemingly anchored to the paper, but is moved ever so slightly from side to side, for a better grip and a clean-cut start.

3. *Stroke*   (3 beats)

   The brush is held in an almost-vertical position as the entire arm is drawn toward the body, advancing toward the lower guide line.

4. *Hold*   (2 beats)

The brush comes to a sudden stop and is for a fleeting moment anchored to the paper, for a clean-cut finish.

5. *Lift*   (1 beat)

The brush is lifted straight up from the paper with the finesse of a pianist lifting his hands from the keyboard.

PRACTICE CAUTIONS

1. In making each stroke, if you want it to be smooth and vigorous, do not think of the guide lines as limiting boundaries. Imagine yourself, instead, to be making a never-ending line, but when you reach the lower boundary come to an abrupt, clean-cut stop.

2. Do not allow a playful hand to turn the regimental strokes of these exercises into strange figures and shapes. Discipline yourself to maintain uniform spaces between strokes. If the exercise calls for slanted strokes, try to maintain the same angle throughout the entire plate.

3. Make a number of strokes. Examine them. Analyze them. Do not "doctor" or touch them up. Weed out the *consistent* faults in these strokes and determine not to repeat these errors. Be your own critic, for continued practice results in habit formation. In order to become a proficient letterer, it is necessary for you to practice, to analyze and correct your errors, and then to practice the corrected strokes. Remember that prac-

tice does not bring *perfection* unless you are practicing the correct thing. It is not a matter of how *much* you practice, but rather how *well* you do it, that really counts in developing good working habits. Therefore, do not just fill reams of paper with haphazard black strokes, and then expect to find improvement. Master each stroke before you go on to the next one.

The following hints may help you discover and correct your mistakes:

1. If you find the end of a stroke is rough and uneven, determine to concentrate on lifting your brush correctly, at the end of the next stroke. Make sure that you do not allow the bristles to drag along the paper.

2. If you find that your strokes are not perfectly perpendicular when they should be, see to it when you resume practice that you sit erect, that you hold your work at a manageable angle, and that you move your entire arm, not only your wrist.

3. If your stroke is shaky, it means that you have been too conscious of the movement of the brush along the paper and have moved it too slowly. This is usually caused by tension, and will be remedied with continued practicing and greater confidence.

PRACTICE PHILOSOPHY

Completing one neat chart of each exercise is by no means sufficient, but the required number of copies cannot be here established in advance; that will vary with your innate lettering ability. Generally speaking, repeat the same exercise just as long as you see signs of improvement; the more the better.

On the whole, let this thought be your guide: Even if you are only practicing on a humble newspaper, you will someday be rewarded for striving for and attaining general neatness, precision, and accuracy. Such self-discipline will at all times carry over from practice work to actual work and is the real secret of the mastery of the art of lettering.

41

42

43

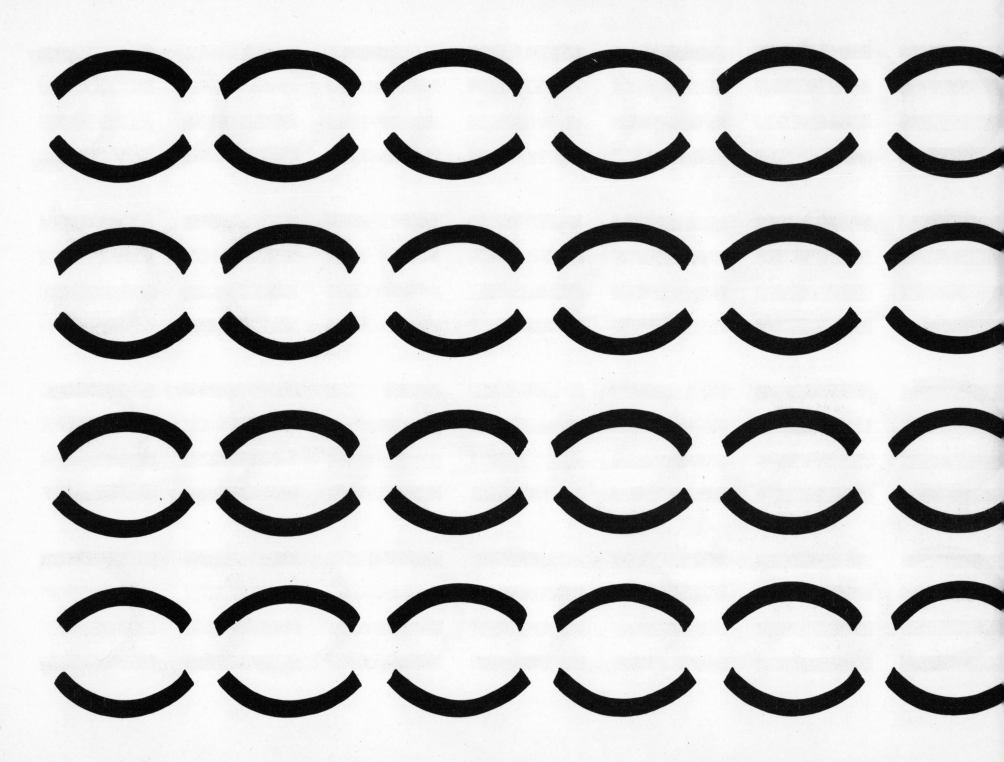

44

CCCCCCCCC

CCCCCCCCC

CCCCCCCCC

CCCCCCCCC

45

S S S S S S S S S

S S S S S S S S S

S S S S S S S S S

S S S S S S S S S

46

47

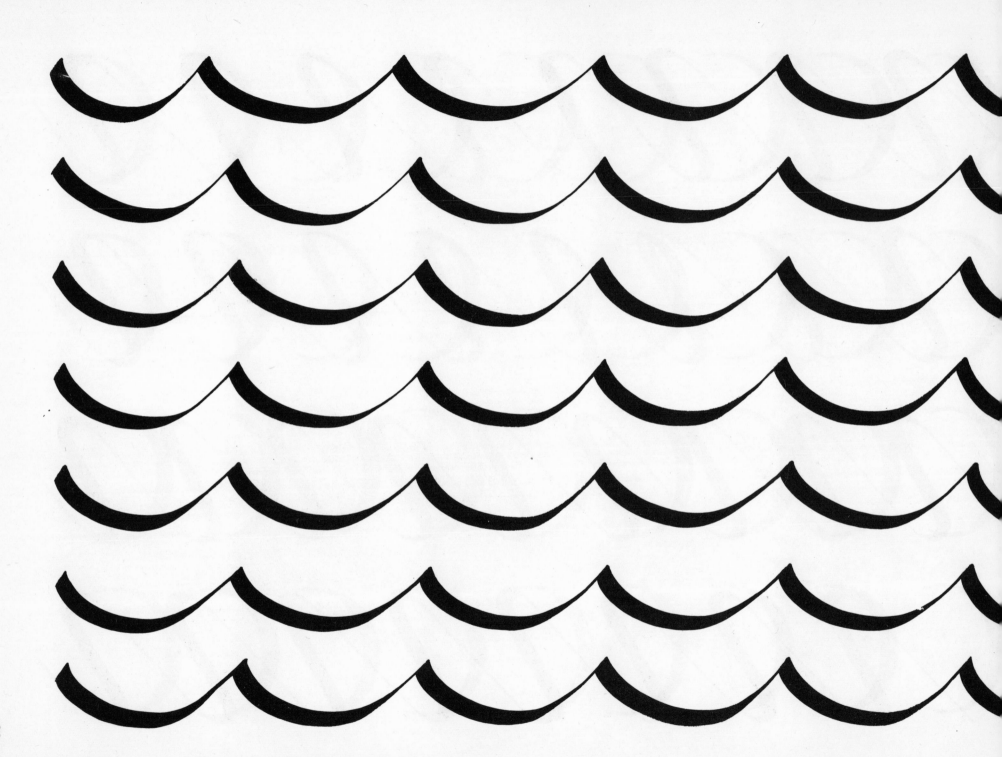

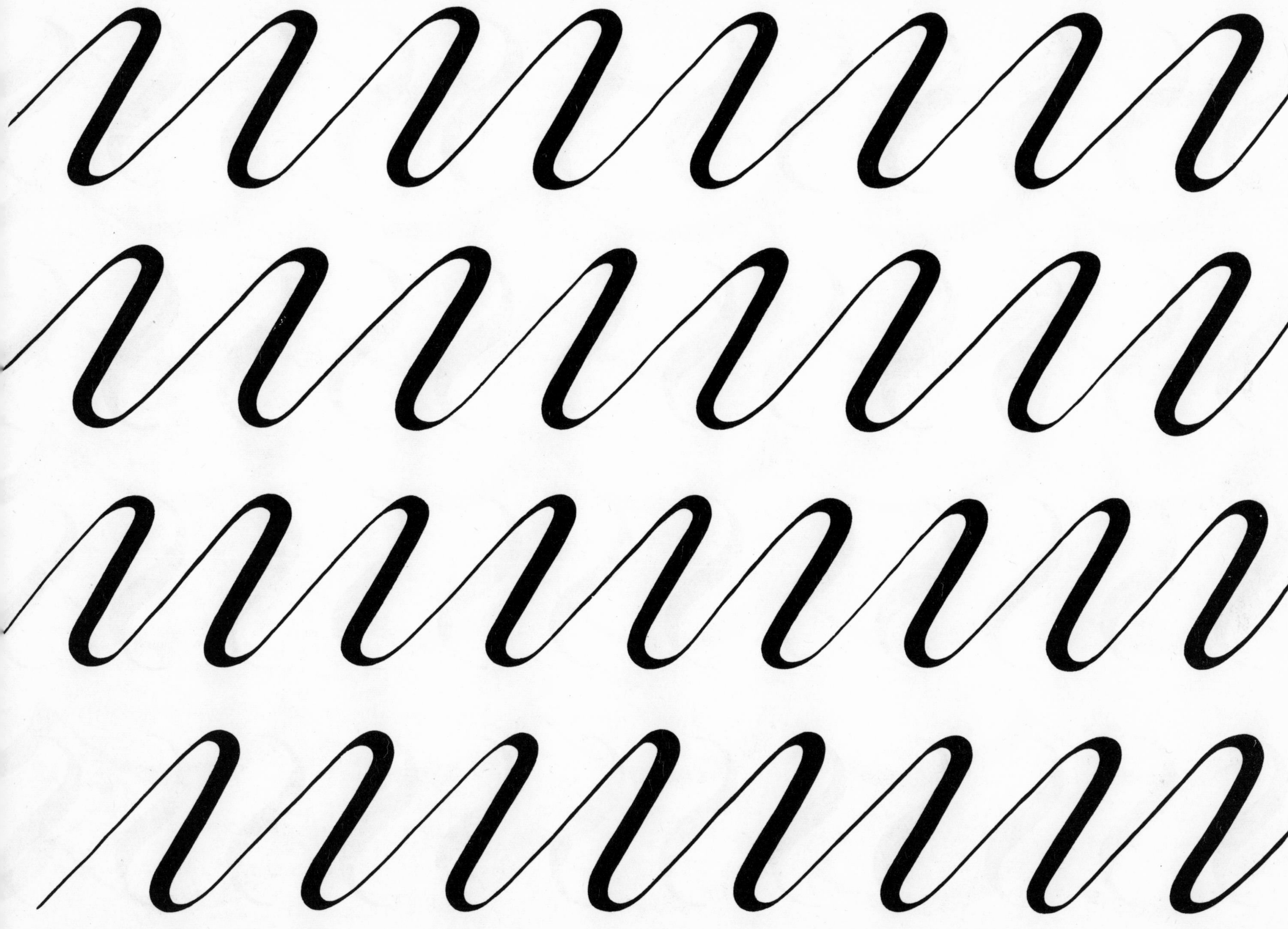

50

Anatomy of Lettering

Now that you know the fundamental strokes, and can manipulate the brush deftly, you are ready to get busy on your first alphabet. Just before you start, study these simple rules carefully; they apply to all lettering you will do:

1. Firm, steady strokes are preferred to short, "choppy" ones.

2. Move the entire arm, not just the wrist or fingers.

3. A complete stroke should be made without having to recharge the brush.

4. When connecting strokes, overlap one on the other, for smooth continuity.

5. Always point the handle of the brush in the same direction as the stroke.

6. Strokes are generally made from top to bottom, and from left to right.

7. Round letters, and letters having pointed vertexes, appear smaller if made just to touch the guide lines. To correct this optical illusion, circles and points of such letters should be extended slightly beyond the guide lines.

The first lettering style for you to try is the single-stroke alphabet, which combines grace and legibility. Since freehand lettering is to a marked degree based on this skeleton style, learning this important structural alphabet will acquaint you with the general anatomy of lettering.

The capital letters of this alphabet, as you will notice, are uniform in thickness but vary in proportion. The letters may, therefore, be classified according to relative proportion:

1. Very narrow
2. Narrow
3. Medium
4. Wide
5. Very wide

In the lower case of this alphabet there isn't the variation in proportion of each letter that is characteristic of the upper case. No set rule can be given as to the relation in height between the lower- and the upper-case letters; the body of the small letter may be anywhere from 1/2 to 2/3 the height of the upper-case letter. This relationship is flexible and may be varied.

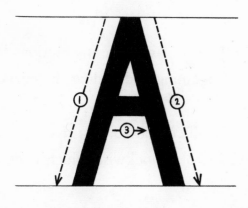

Medium, 3 Strokes

1. Going from top to bottom, make left diagonal.
2. Starting at top, make right diagonal.
3. Going from left to right, make horizontal crossbar.

   The crossbar is made rather high up, giving this letter a graceful, haughty appearance. The A should be well balanced and symmetrical, and should appear to be standing squarely on both feet. An imaginary line dropped from the apex should divide the pyramid into two equal parts.

Narrow, 4 Strokes

1. Going from top to bottom, make a vertical stem.
2. Starting at top of the stem, and pivoting the brush slightly between the fingers, execute the upper loop so that it ends at center or slightly above center of the stem.
3. Starting where upper loop ended, and using the brush similarly, describe the greater part of the lower loop.
4. Starting at bottom of stem, make a curved stroke to meet and overlap on stroke 3.

   The B looks best when the loops are narrow. The lower loop is generally larger and proportionately wider than the upper loop. Each loop should form a narrow, symmetrical and small D.

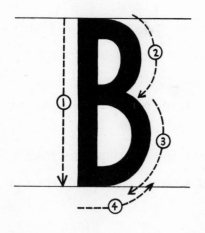

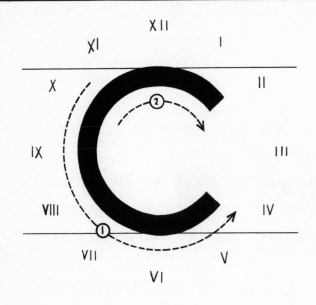

Very Wide, 2 Strokes

For the letter C, and for all round letters to follow, we shall clarify the instructions by using the analogy of a clock to designate the points of beginning and ending the curved strokes.

1. From 10:30, make a curved stroke counter clockwise which ends at about 4:30.
2. From 10:00 (allowing for an overlap), make a curved stroke clockwise which ends at about 2:00.

The C looks best when it is full and round. It should extend slightly beyond the guide lines.

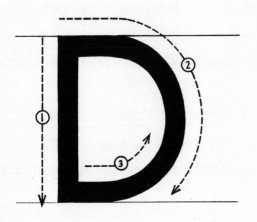

Wide, 3 Strokes

1. Going from top to bottom, make a vertical stem.
2. Starting at top of the stem, and pivoting the brush slightly between the fingers, make a downward curve until it almost reaches the guide line.
3. Starting at bottom of stem, make an upward curve to meet and overlap on stroke 2.

The white space, or counter, in the D should also present a pleasing shape to the eye.

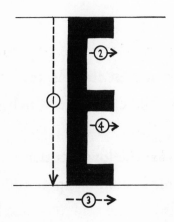

Very Narrow, 4 Strokes

1. Going from top to bottom, make a vertical stem.
2. Starting at top of the stem, and going from left to right, make a short horizontal, flush with the upper guide line.
3. Starting at bottom of the stem, and going from left to right, make a short horizontal along the lower guide line, the same length as stroke 2.
4. Starting from about center of the stem, and going from left to right, make another horizontal of the same length.

   The E looks best when it is made narrow. The middle crossbar may be slightly above the center.

Very Narrow, 3 Strokes

1. Going from top to bottom, make a vertical stem.
2. Starting at top of the stem, and going from left to right, make a short horizontal, flush with the upper guide line.
3. Starting at about center of the stem, and going from left to right, make another horizontal of the same length.

   The F is similar to the E except that it lacks the bottom horizontal, and the crossbar may be made slightly below the center.

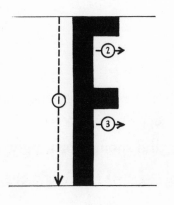

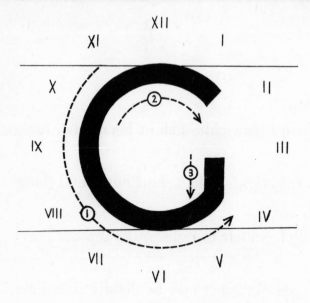

Very Wide, 3 Strokes

Using the clock analogy again:

1. From 10:30, make a curved stroke counterclockwise which ends at about 4:30.
2. From 10:00 (allowing for an overlap), make a curved stroke clockwise which ends at about 1:30.
3. Going from top to bottom, make a short vertical stem to join the lower curve.

The G is similar to the C except for the short vertical stem. It should appear full bodied and well balanced.

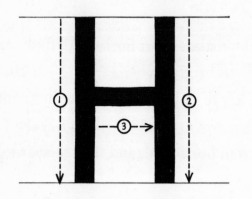

Wide, 3 Strokes

1. Going from top to bottom, make a vertical stem.
2. Going from top to bottom some distance away, make a stem parallel to the first one.
3. Going from left to right, make a horizontal crossbar to connect the two verticals.

The crossbar should be drawn at about or above the center, and should form right angles where it meets the verticals.

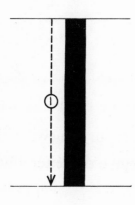

Very Narrow, 1 Stroke

1. Going from top to bottom, make a vertical stem.

   The I is similar to the practice stroke on page 41. It is a mistake to put a dot over the capital I.

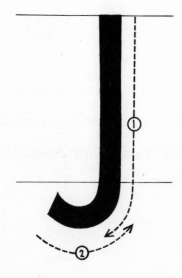

Very Narrow, 2 Strokes

1. Going from top to bottom, make a vertical stem, and end it with a short hook-curve to the left.

2. Going from left to right, draw a slightly curved line to meet and overlap on stroke 1.

   The J may be made either with the curved hook well below or resting on the lower guide line.

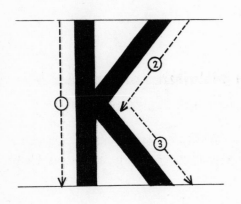

Narrow, 3 Strokes

1. Going from top to bottom, make a vertical stem.

2. Going from top to bottom, make the upper diagonal.

3. From the point where stroke 2 ends, draw the lower diagonal.

   In the K, the joining of the two diagonals should be at the center or somewhat above the center of the stem. The lower diagonal should extend so as to give the letter a wide base.

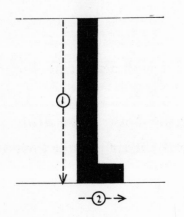

Very Narrow, 2 Strokes

1. Going from top to bottom, make a vertical stem.

2. Going from left to right, starting at the bottom of the stem, make a short horizontal.

   In the L, the horizontal should rest directly on the guide line.

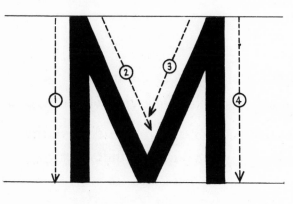

Very Wide, 4 Strokes

1. Going from top to bottom, make a vertical stem.
2. Going from top to bottom, make a diagonal to the lower guide line.
3. Going from top to bottom, make a diagonal to meet the first one in a vertex.
4. Going from top to bottom, make a vertical stem.

The two diagonals in the center of the M should form a perfect V. The areas on either side of the center V should be equal.

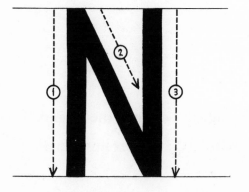

Medium, 3 Strokes

1. Going from top to bottom, make a vertical stem.
2. Going from top to bottom, make a diagonal to the lower guide line.
3. Going from top to bottom, make a vertical stem to meet the end of the diagonal.

The areas formed on either side of the diagonal should be equal. This is an indication that the letter is well balanced.

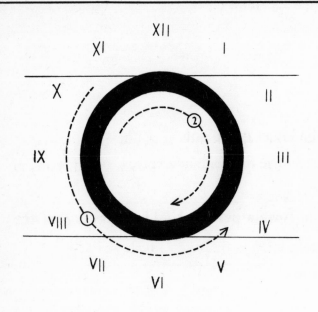

Very Wide, 2 Strokes

Using the clock analogy again:

1. From 10:30, make a curved stroke counterclockwise which ends at about 4:30.

2. From 10:00 (allowing for an overlap), make a curved stroke clockwise which ends at about 5:00.

The O should be optically round. It should extend slightly beyond the guide lines.

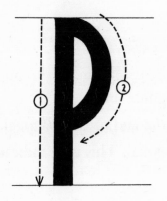

Narrow, 2 Strokes

1. Going from top to bottom, make a vertical stem.

2. Starting at top of the stem, and pivoting the brush slightly between the fingers, make a narrow loop ending a little below the center of the stem.

The P is similar to the R, which is to follow.

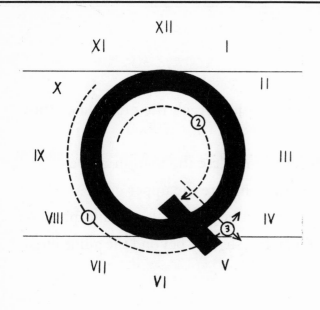

Very Wide, 3 Strokes

Using the clock analogy again:

1. From 10:30, make a curved stroke counterclockwise which ends at about 4:30.

2. From 10:00 (allowing for an overlap), make a curved stroke clockwise which ends at about 5:00.

3. Going from top to bottom, make a short diagonal through the lower right arc of the circle, and extend it a little below the lower guide line.

The Q should extend a little beyond the guide lines.

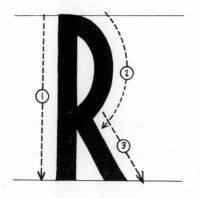

Narrow, 3 Strokes

1. Going from top to bottom, make a vertical stem.

2. Starting at the top of the stem, and pivoting the brush slightly between the fingers, make a narrow loop ending a little below the center of the stem.

3. From the point where stroke 2 ends, draw a diagonal to extend beyond the loop, and form a wide base.

The R is similar to the P, plus the diagonal or tail.

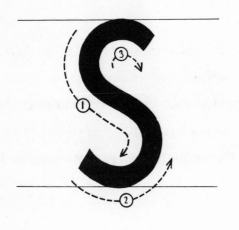

Medium, 3 Strokes

1. Going from top to bottom, make a compound curve to just reach the guide line. (See page 46.)
2. Going from left to right, and allowing for an overlap, complete the bottom curve.
3. Going from left to right, and allowing for an overlap, complete the upper curve.

   In the S, the bottom curve, which forms the base, should be slightly larger and proportionately wider than the upper curve. The S should extend slightly beyond the guide lines.

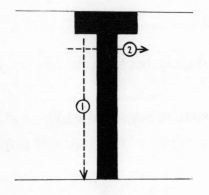

Narrow, 2 Strokes

1. Going from top to bottom, make a vertical stem.
2. Going from left to right, make a short horizontal crossbar along the upper guide line.

   For a well-balanced T, the cross stroke on one side of the stem should be optically equal to that on the other side; the stem acting as a fulcrum.

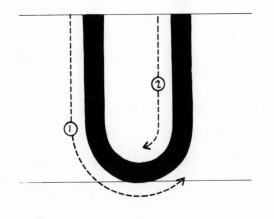

Wide, 2 Strokes

1. Going from top to bottom, make a vertical stem; just before reaching the lower guide line, swing into a curve to the right.
2. Going from top to bottom, make a vertical, and complete the curve, overlapping on stroke 1. The U may be pictorially described as looking like a hammock suspended from two uprights. The semicircular base should be perfectly balanced, and should extend slightly beyond the guide line.

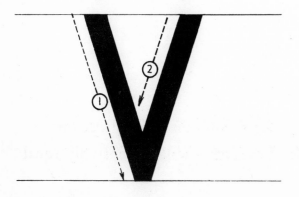

Medium, 2 Strokes

1. Going from top to bottom, make the left diagonal.
2. Going from top to bottom, make right diagonal to meet the first in a vertex.
An imaginary line drawn perpendicular to the base from the vertex of the V should divide the white area into two equal parts.

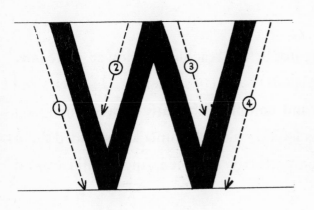

Very Wide, 4 Strokes

1. Going from top to bottom, make a diagonal.

2. Going from top to bottom, make a diagonal to meet the first one.

3. Going from top to bottom, repeat stroke 1.

4. Going from top to bottom, make a diagonal to meet stroke 3.

The W is really a combination of two slightly narrower-than-normal V's.

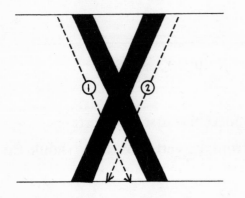

Narrow, 2 Strokes

1. Going from top to bottom, make a diagonal from left to right.

2. Going from top to bottom, make a diagonal to cross through the first one.

The lower half of the X may be a trifle wider than the upper half. The intersection should be slightly above the center.

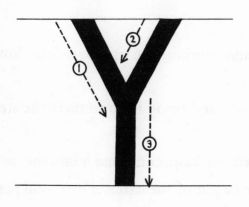

Medium, 3 Strokes

1. Going from top to bottom, make a short diagonal.
2. Going from top to bottom, make a diagonal to meet the end of stroke 1, and form a small v.
3. From the junction point of the diagonals, make a vertical to the lower guide line.
   The short stem of the Y should extend from the vertex of the small v, balancing the two diagonals.

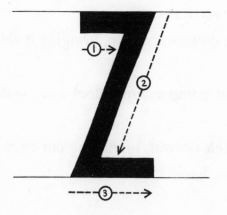

Narrow, 3 Strokes

1. Going from left to right, make a horizontal along the upper guide line.
2. Going from top to bottom, make a diagonal.
3. Going from left to right, make a horizontal along the lower guide line.
   The lower horizontal should be slightly larger than the upper one, to give the Z a wide base.

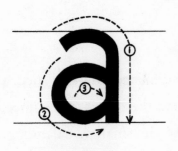

3 Strokes

1. Starting a little below the waist line, describe an arc, and continue the stroke straight down to the base line to form a stem.

2. Going counterclockwise, make the bottom of the loop, and bring it up to meet the stem slightly above the base line.

3. Going clockwise and overlapping on stroke 2, complete the loop, and blend it into the stem. The loop of the a should be slightly more than ½ the height of the letter. The round parts should extend slightly beyond the guide lines.

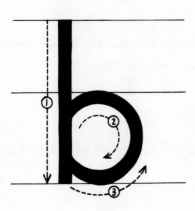

3 Strokes

1. Going from the ascender line to the base line, make a vertical stem.

2. Starting at the stem a little below the waist line, make a downward loop, bringing it almost to the base line.

3. Starting at the stem slightly above the base line, and going counterclockwise, make a curved stroke to meet and overlap on stroke 2.

The body or loop of the b should be an incomplete circle or oval, branching out from the stem. The loop should extend slightly beyond the guide lines.

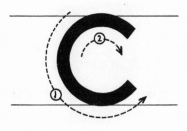

2 Strokes

Remembering the clock analogy:

1. From 10:30, make a curved stroke counterclockwise which ends at about 4:30.
2. From 10:00 (allowing for an overlap), make a curved stroke clockwise which ends at about 2:00.

The c should be optically round, and should extend slightly beyond the guide lines.

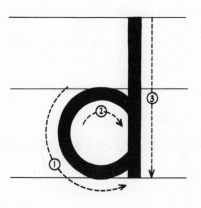

3 Strokes

Remembering the clock analogy:

1. From 10:30, make a curved stroke counterclockwise which ends at about 4:30.
2. From 10:00 (allowing for an overlap), make a curved stroke clockwise which ends at about 2:00.
3. Starting at the ascender line and going down, make a vertical stem, joining the curve, and extending to the base line.

The d is really b looking at itself in the mirror. The body of this letter extends slightly beyond the guide lines.

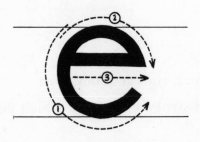

3 Strokes

Remembering the clock analogy:

1. From 10:30, make a curved stroke counterclockwise which ends at about 4:00.

2. From 10:00 (allowing for an overlap), make a curved stroke which ends at about 2:30.

3. Going from left to right, make a horizontal crossbar slightly above center.

The e looks like c with a crossbar. It extends slightly beyond the guide lines.

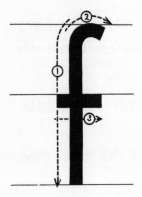

3 Strokes

1. Starting at the ascender line with a slight hook, make a vertical stem to the base line.

2. Allowing for an overlap on stroke 1, and going clockwise, complete the curve.

3. Going from left to right, make a crossbar just under the waist line.

The right side of the crossbar of the f may be made slightly longer than the left side. The curve extends slightly beyond the cap line.

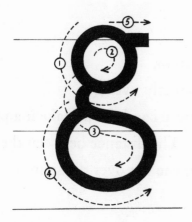

5 Strokes

Remembering the clock analogy:

Strokes 1 and 2 follow the procedure for the letter o.

3. Starting on the circle at 7:00, and extending from the circle, make a compound curve, ending it at about 5:00.

4. Starting at the left side of the compound curve a little above the base line, and going counterclockwise, complete the base loop with the necessary overlap.

5. From the circle at 1:00, extend a short crossbar, going from left to right.

The upper circle is about halfway down between the waist line and the base line, and extends well beyond the waist line. The base loop should be centered directly under the circle.

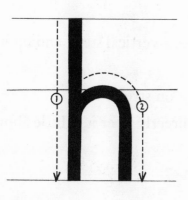

2 Strokes

1. Going from the ascender line to the base line, make a vertical stem.

2. Starting at the stem a little below the waist line, and going clockwise, make an arc. Without lifting the brush, continue the stroke to the base line.

The arc of the h extends slightly above the waist line. The h resembles n with the stem extended to the cap line.

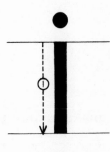

1 Stroke and Dot

1. Going from the waist line to the base line, make a vertical stem.

   Put a round dot of the same optical thickness as the stem, directly over it.

   For some strange reason, beginners often omit the dot over the i and the j. Make it a point to check up and see that you are not guilty of this omission. The distance between the dot and the stroke is not mathematically fixed. Be sure to center the dot over the stem.

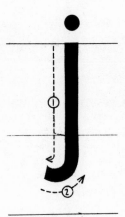

2 Strokes and Dot

1. Going from the waist line to well below the base line, make a vertical stem, ending it with a slight hook.

2. Going counterclockwise, complete this hook, overlapping on stroke 1.

   Put a round dot of the same optical thickness as the stem directly over it, a little above the stem.

   The j is really i with a lower extension and hook.

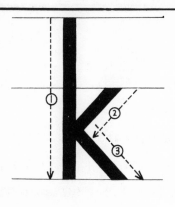

3 Strokes

1. Going from the ascender line to the base line, make a vertical stem.
2. Starting at the waist line and going down diagonally, make the upper arm.
3. From the point where stroke 2 ends, and going down diagonally, make the lower arm.
   The meeting of the arms on the stem should be at about the center between waist and base lines. The lower diagonal should extend a little beyond the upper one on the base line, to give stability to the letter.

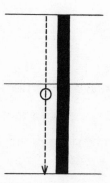

1 Stroke

1. Going from the ascender line to the base line, make a vertical stem.
   This letter is exactly like a capital I, or like stroke 1 of the k you have just made.

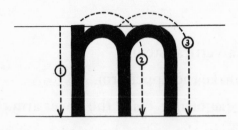

3 Strokes

1. Going from the waist line to the base line, make a vertical stem.
2. Starting a little below the waist line and going clockwise, make an arc and straighten into a line parallel to the stem, going to the base line.
3. Repeat step 2.

Make sure that all three vertical strokes are parallel and equidistant. Both arcs should look the same. The curves should extend slightly beyond the waist line.

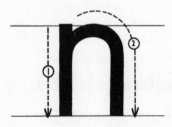

2 Strokes

1. Going from the waist line to the base line, make a vertical stem.
2. Starting a little below the waist line and going clockwise, make an arc and straighten it into a line parallel to the stem.

The n is somewhat wider than a single section of the m. The curve should extend slightly beyond the waist line.

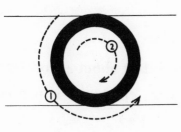

2 Strokes

Remembering the clock analogy:

1. From 10:30, make a curved stroke counterclockwise which ends at about 4:30.
2. From 10:00 (allowing for an overlap), make a curved stroke clockwise which ends at about 5:00.

The o should extend slightly beyond the guide lines. It is made exactly like the capital O, within the lower-case dimensions.

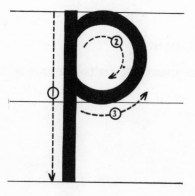

3 Strokes

1. Going from the waist line to the descender line, make a vertical stem.
2. Starting at the stem slightly below the waist line, and going clockwise, make a partial loop.
3. Starting at the stem slightly above the base line, and going counterclockwise, complete the loop, and overlap on stroke 2.

The loop of the p extends slightly beyond the guide lines. This letter is like b except that it has a descender instead of an ascender.

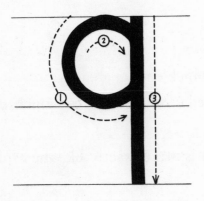

3 Strokes

Remembering the clock analogy:

1. From 10:30, make a curved stroke counterclockwise which ends at about 4:30.
2. From 10:00 (allowing for an overlap), make a curved stroke clockwise which ends at about 2:00.
3. Going from the waist line to the descender line, make a vertical stem.

   The letter q is like p facing the other way.

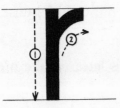

2 Strokes

1. Going from the waist line to the base line, make a vertical stem.
2. Starting at the stem, slightly below the waist line, extend a short arc to form an ear.

   The ear of the r should blend smoothly into the stem.

3 Strokes

1. Starting at the waist line and going down, make a compound curve to just reach the base line.

2. Starting slightly above the base line and going counterclockwise, complete the bottom curve, overlapping on stroke 1.

3. Starting at stroke 1 and allowing for an overlap, make a curved stroke clockwise to complete the upper curve.

The s should extend slightly beyond the guide lines. It is made exactly like the capital S, within the lower-case dimensions.

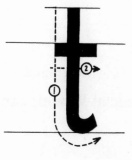

2 Strokes

1. Going from the "t" line toward the base line, make a vertical stem, ending it with a slight hook.

2. Going from left to right, make a crossbar just under the waist line.

Note that the ascender of the t is shorter than that of other letters having ascenders. The right side of the crossbar may be made a little longer than the left.

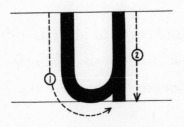

2 Strokes

1. Going from the waist line to the base line, make a vertical stem, swinging it around counterclockwise just above the base line, to form an arc.
2. Going from the waist line to the base line, make a vertical stem to meet the arc, and extend to the base line.

A u is really an inverted n.

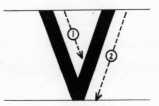

2 Strokes

1. Going from the waist line to the base line, make the left diagonal.
2. Going from the waist line to the base line, make the right diagonal, to meet the first in a vertex.

An imaginary line drawn perpendicular to the base from the vertex should divide the white area into two equal parts. The v is made exactly like the capital V, within the lower-case dimensions.

76

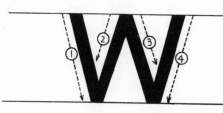

4 Strokes

1. Going from the waist line to the base line, make a diagonal.
2. Going from the waist line to the base line, make a diagonal to meet the first in a vertex.
3. Going from the waist line to the base line, repeat stroke 1.
4. Going from the waist line to the base line, make a diagonal to meet stroke 3.
   The w is really a combination of two slightly narrower-than-normal v's. It is made exactly like the capital W, within the lower-case dimensions.

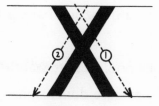

2 Strokes

1. Going from the waist line to the base line, make a diagonal from left to right.
2. Going from the waist line to the base line, make a diagonal to cross through the first one. The intersection should be slightly above center. The lower half of the x may be a trifle wider than the upper half. This letter is made exactly like the capital X, within the lower-case dimensions.

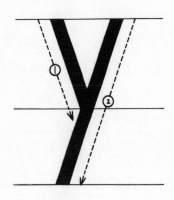

2 Strokes

1. Going from the waist line to the base line, make the left diagonal.
2. Going from the waist line to the base line, make the right diagonal extending it to the descender line.

The y is really v with the right diagonal extended to form a descender.

3 Strokes

1. Going from left to right, make a horizontal along the waist line.
2. Starting at the end of stroke 1, make a diagonal to the base line.
3. Going from left to right, starting at the end of stroke 2, make a horizontal along the base line.

The lower horizontal should be slightly larger than the upper one, to give stability to the letter. The z is made exactly like the capital Z, within the lower-case dimensions.

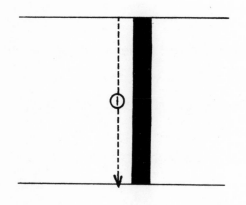

1 Stroke

1. Going from the cap line to the base line, make a vertical.

   The number 1 is made exactly like the capital I.

2 Strokes

1. Starting a little below the cap line, make a curve clockwise; then, continuing the stroke down and toward the left, end it at the base line.

2. From the point where stroke 1 ends, and going from left to right, draw a horizontal along the base line.

   The curve of the 2 should extend slightly beyond the guide line.

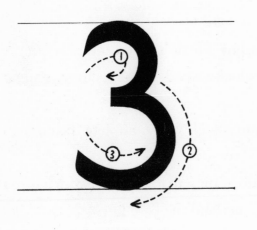

3 Strokes

1. Starting a little below the cap line, and going clockwise, make the upper loop, ending it slightly above center.
2. From the point where stroke 1 ends, describe another loop, larger than the first, carrying it through to the base line.
3. Starting a little above the base line, and going counterclockwise, complete the curve, and overlap on stroke 2.

The number 3 should extend slightly beyond the guide lines.

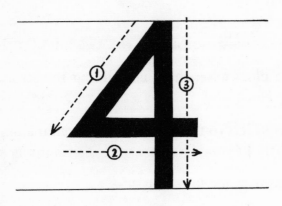

3 Strokes

1. Starting at the cap line, make a diagonal, ending a little below center.
2. From the point where stroke 1 ends, and going from left to right, make a horizontal parallel to the guide lines.
3. From the initial starting point, make a vertical to the base line.

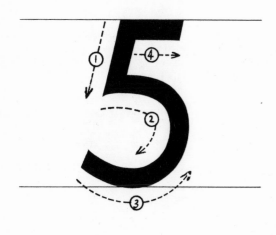

4 Strokes

1. Starting at the cap line, make a short diagonal, ending a little above center.
2. From the point where stroke 1 ends, and going clockwise, describe a curve, ending it at the base line.
3. Starting a little above the base line and going counterclockwise, complete the curve, over-lapping on stroke 2.
4. From the initial starting point, make a horizontal along the cap line, going from left to right. The bottom curve of the 5 should extend slightly beyond the base line.

2 Strokes

1. Starting at the cap line and going counterclockwise, describe a curve, extending it until a little beyond the point of contact with the base line.
2. From about the center of stroke 1 and going clockwise, make a curve to complete the small circle and overlap on stroke 1.
   The bottom curve of the 6 should extend slightly beyond the base line. The number 6 is really a small circle with an extending arm.

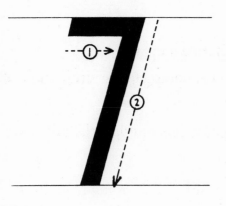

2 Strokes

1. Going from left to right along the cap line, make a short horizontal.
2. From the point where stroke 1 ends, make a diagonal to the base line.

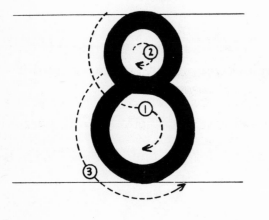

3 Strokes

1. Starting at the cap line, describe a compound curve as in the letter s.
2. Overlapping the beginning of stroke 1 and going clockwise, complete the upper circle.
3. Going counterclockwise, complete the lower circle, overlapping on stroke 1.
   The lower circle of the 8, which is directly under the upper one, is larger and proportionately wider than the upper one. The number 8 extends slightly beyond the guide lines.

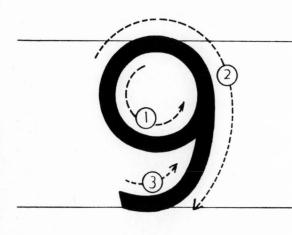

3 Strokes

1. Starting at the cap line and going counterclockwise, describe a curve.
2. Overlapping the beginning of stroke 1 and going clockwise, complete the circle and extend the curve to the base line.
3. Starting a little above the base line and going counterclockwise, complete the tail.
   The number 9 extends slightly beyond the guide lines.

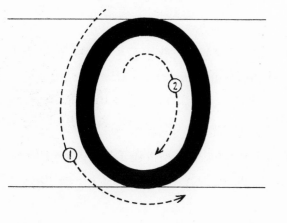

2 Strokes

1. Starting a little below the cap line and going counterclockwise, describe a curve until it meets the base line.
2. Overlapping on the beginning of stroke 1 and going clockwise, complete the oval, overlapping on the end of stroke 1.
   The O should extend beyond the guide lines.

1 Stroke and Dot

1. Starting a little below the cap line and going clockwise, describe a compound curve.
   Place the dot in the optical center, resting on the base line and extending slightly below it.

5 Strokes

1. Starting a little below the cap line and going counterclockwise, describe a curve, ending it slightly above center.
2. Overlapping stroke 1, make a similar curve of greater proportion, ending it at the base line.
3. Starting well above the base line, and going clockwise, complete the curve, overlapping on stroke 2.
4. Make the horizontal, resting on stroke 3.
5. Overlapping the beginning of stroke 1 and going clockwise, complete the upper curve. The & extends slightly beyond the guide lines.

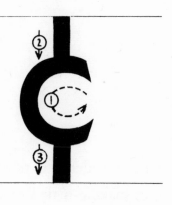

3 Strokes

1. Make a small curve.
2. From the cap line make a short vertical to reach the upper part of the curve.
3. From the under part of the curve, and directly underneath the upper vertical, make a short vertical to reach the base line.

The ¢ sign is like a small c with interrupted verticals.

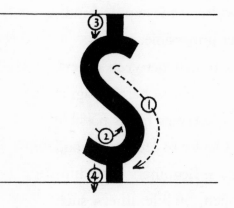

4 Strokes

1. Make a compound curve.
2. Going counterclockwise, complete the lower curve.
3. From the cap line make a short vertical to reach the upper curve.
4. From the lower curve and directly underneath the upper vertical, make a short vertical to reach the base line.

The $ sign is like a small s with interrupted verticals.

Spacing

C H A P T E R   6

Once having acquired the skill to do individual letters, consideration must be given to the proper grouping or spacing of letters and words. Proper spacing makes easy reading, whereas inconsistent or staccato spacing makes the reader more conscious of the letters than of the message they spell out.

If the shape of each letter were based on a square block, spacing would offer no special problem. It would merely be a matter of measuring off equal distances between blocks, and setting the letters into these cubicles. However, the variety in widths and shapes of individual letters makes the allotment of an arbitrary space for each letter impossible.

To space words correctly, be guided by the blank optical area between letters, not by distances measured off on a guide line. An analogy may be found helpful here. Imagine the spaces between the letters of a word to be filled with a liquid, and try as far as possible to equalize the area which the eye must swim in order to read from letter to letter. In good spacing, there appears to be the same amount of liquid between letters. Beginners have difficulty with spacing because certain letters, such as L and T, are "open," while others, such as N and H, are "closed."

Accepting the above analogy:

In Fig. A there would be considerably more liquid flowing between the L and the A than between the I and the N. The letters in this figure are of the same width (except, of course, the I) and the space between letters was equally measured off by linear distance on the guide line. Such mechanical spacing is considered poor.

PLAYING

A

In Fig. B the spacing is improved, because the proportions of the letters have been varied. This change is particularly obvious in the shortening of the crossbar on the L, which allows the A to come closer and fill the "ocean" between this unfortunate combination of letters. The space between letters is still measured mathematically. Owing to the change in the proportions of the letters, the relative volume between letters has been altered, although not entirely equalized. There still is less liquid between the I and the N than between the L and the A. This word is not well spaced.

PLAYING

B

B

PLAYING

C

In Fig. C the word is well spaced. The proportions of the letters remain as in Fig. B and the spacing between letters is optically correct rather than mathematically equal. There seems to be an equal volume of liquid flowing between letters and this, according to our analogy, is an indication of proper spacing.

PROCEDURE FOR SPACING

1. For practical show-card or poster work, rule in the guide lines of the determined height, and with soft pencil, chalk, or charcoal lay out the lettering rapidly in single,

skeleton strokes. In this sketchy ghost lettering, you should be more concerned with spacing than with the perfection of each letter.

2. When laying out your copy, do not stay too close to the lettering surface. It is better for the eye to be able to span the whole word and its effect, and not just concentrate on isolated letters. To work too closely is in many cases not to see the forest because of the trees.

3. With the copy thus roughly laid out, begin to brush in the letters. Do not feel compelled to follow the skeleton plan slavishly. As you brush in the letters, feel free to improve the spacing wherever possible.

4. For freehand work it is best to brush in the lettering rapidly, since the less hesitantly a line of lettering is done the more natural the spacing will be. In making rapid strokes, the eye scans the entire line at one time, and projects a mental image of the complete row of lettering. This aids in correct spacing.

5. The beginner may deem it advisable to play safe; that is, to correct the rough ghost lettering and spacing before using his brush. Of course, the more experienced the letterer is the less he relies on preliminary layout and correction work. His spacing will be as spontaneous as the natural spacing of handwriting is to a good penman.

6. Consistency in spacing is an important consideration. "Tight" spacing is just as culpable

as "extended" spacing, if either measure is resorted to to "justify" a line. Obvious "squeezing in" of a few extra letters at the end of a line is no more pardonable than stretching out the last few letters. This telescoping or expanding, if it becomes obvious to the reader, re-creates for him the letterer's predicament.

RHYTHM IN SPACING

Good spacing may be considered not only from the point of view of areas between letters, but also the space within letters. Owing to the varying proportions of letter forms, and the recurrence of certain shapes and white areas in a mass of lettering, a pleasing sense of rhythm is established. Miss Sallie B. Tannahill, who has experimented with lettering from the point of view of texture and pattern, has evolved some excellent designs, shown in her *P's and Q's of Lettering*.

The figure above shows the effect of the rhythmic repetition of round letter forms flanked by narrow ones. The role that the white paper plays in the completed picture is here aptly demonstrated.

Reproduction Lettering

TO BE GOOD enough someday to do lettering for reproduction is the aspiration of many a poster letterer. It calls for a knowledge of basic letter forms, skillful use of lettering tools, and preciseness of technique.

MATERIALS

Brushes and Pens—A good quality show-card brush will be found serviceable for reproduction work. Of course, the smaller or finer the lettering the smaller the brush to be used. For extra-fine lettering, requiring delicate serifs or hairlines, a long pointed rigger brush is best. Riggers are used also for script lettering, outlines, scrolls, and general touching up.

There is a wide range of pen sizes for reproduction lettering, including hairline crow-quill pens and the entire family of Speedball pens shown on page 15. Lettering pens, as a rule, work best on smooth stock, and are used not only to produce small lettering, but to "sharpen up" broad lettering.

Ruling Pens—The instrument shown on page 15 is used for inking in straight lines of any thickness, and works best on a smooth surface. The width of the lines is regulated by means of a side-adjusting screw, which enables you to set the blades closer or wider apart. The farther apart the blades the wider the resulting line. Since the side-screw fixes and locks the position of the blades, the lines ruled in with the pen will be of uniform width.

The ruling pen is filled by means of a brush charged with India ink, applied to the space between the blades. Before using the pen, always stroke it on trial scrap paper to see whether the pen is functioning properly and to check whether the line is of the desired width. In running the pen along a ruler, hold the ruling pen vertically and make certain that the side with the adjusting screw faces away from the ruler. Always clean your ruling pen after use by washing the blades with cold water and wiping them perfectly dry. This will prevent the caking of the lettering fluid in the reservoir. Take care not to drop the pen, as that will damage the fine tips of the blades.

Compasses—Compasses are used freely in reproduction work for designs and lettering. For circles up to three inches, there are bow compasses with pencil and pen attachments, for making perfect circles in pencil or ink. The best bow compasses are those which have an adjusting wheel in the center of the fork to regulate the size of the circle and to keep the blades firm. Compasses also are available for making larger circles. These are regulated by merely spreading the forks to the desired radius.

Compasses with an adjusting wheel, whenever they can be used, are preferable, since once the radius is determined it can be set or fixed rigidly.

The ink attachment for the compasses is controlled similarly to that for the ruling pen. It can be adjusted so that the pen will make lines of varied thicknesses. It is virtually a small ruling pen attached to a compass, made to produce circles in ink.

When describing an ink circle with a compass, handle your instrument on the grooved fulcrum on top, and apply as little pressure as possible on the side bearing the ink attachment. Be sure that the needle point is kept fine and sharp, for if it is blunted it will produce a large pivoting hole in your working surface. The compasses should be cared for and cleaned exactly the same way as the ruling pen.

Rulers—For ruling lines, use a beveled, metal-edged ruler whose edge does not come in direct contact with the paper. If such a ruler is not available, and you resort to a flat ruler or straightedge, be sure to tip the pen a little away from the ruler. Failure to do so may make the ink creep underneath the ruler, causing smears and runs.

Working Surfaces—For best results, illustration or Bristol board should be used. When a brush is used for lettering, a rough-grained board with a slight "tooth" will give the best results. Where the pen or compass is used, a kid-finish, that is, a smooth-finish, board will make sharper lines possible.

Working Procedure—Lettering for reproduction involves great responsibility on the part of the artist. His master copy will be duplicated in quantity and the "accidentals" that might be overlooked in an individual card are not tolerated in originals for reproduction.

Great pains are, therefore, taken to make the master copy as perfect as possible. The following is a step-by-step outline of the procedure for creating lettering for reproduction:

1. Pencil in the lettering roughly on white cardboard. Be more concerned with character and good spacing than with perfection of shape.

2. Trace the lettering onto tracing paper with a hard pencil, at the same time making improvements and alterations as seen fit. This provides another opportunity for improving spacing and judging the effect of the completed lettering job.

3. Turn the tracing paper over, and with a soft pencil black in the area directly underneath the lettering.

4. Place the tracing in position on Bristol or illustration board, and affix it firmly with Scotch tape.

5. With a hard lead pencil (3H) sharpened to a fine point carefully trace in the outlines of the letters. Do not dig in or you will form irremovable ridges on the board. Lift a corner of the paper to see if the tracing is coming through properly.

6. Remove the tracing paper, and lightly rub over the lettering on the board with a kneaded eraser or the broad edge of a piece of art gum, to leave a faint impression of the tracing.

7. With a well-sharpened semihard (2H) pencil, go over the faint outlines of the letters,

still making necessary corrections, to give you the lettering in its final outline, ready for paint or ink.

8. When using the brush, carefully paint in each letter completely before going on to the next one. The procedure is different, however, when a ruling pen is used. Here, you *outline* the letters by inking in all the verticals first, using triangle and T square. Then ink in all the horizontals and diagonals. Now ink in all the curves and circles. When the copy is thus completely outlined, fill in the letters with a brush or pen of appropriate size, using black India ink or black poster color. Care must be taken not to go beyond the outlines, and at the same time not to leave any "holidays," or white spaces, as they will show up badly in the reproduction.

9. When the color is dry, pass the eraser over the entire surface to remove pencil lines, tracing smudges, or fingerprints.

10. Check carefully for sharpness and accuracy. An enlarging glass may be used to detect minute ragged edges.

11. For touching-up purposes, where it is necessary to sharpen edges or correct slight discrepancies, use opaque white poster color. However, try to avoid excessive touching up, as that is an admission of a struggle, and shows poor technique.

12. A mat of eggshell board may be used to enhance the appearance of the finished work.

Whether or not a mat is used, a paper flap should be placed over the work for protection. The job is now ready to be submitted.

It is not to be inferred that all commercial reproduction lettering is turned out by means of this lengthy procedure. The extent of the routine depends upon the skill of the letterer and the nature of the lettering job. It is not unusual to see an expert letterer pencil in his copy roughly directly on the illustration board, color it immediately, and do a good job to boot! The student, however, will not go amiss if he plays safe and follows the outlined procedure until he gains in experience and confidence.

It should be remembered that lettering for reproduction does not necessarily have to be painted in the size it will appear when finally printed. As a rule, it is easier to work on a larger scale, since greater detail is made possible without eyestrain. Thus, when making an original for a letterhead, it may be made twice the finished size. By the same token, if commissioned to design reproduction lettering for work of unusually large dimensions, it may be drawn just as small as is convenient. In each instance, blue pencil marks should indicate the size of the reduction or enlargement for the benefit of the photoengraver.

Lettering made large in the original and reduced by the photoengraver will in most cases appear sharper and cleaner than the original. One must take care not to make thin lines so fine that they will disappear when reduced. For previewing a lettering job that is to be reduced, a diminishing glass will be found handy.

S E R I E S   O F

Alphabets

C H A P T E R   8

Single thick, single stroke

THIS is the first alphabet that the student of lettering should undertake. It provides a good study of the elementary shapes and strokes of all letter forms, and at the same time is a practical style for many and varied purposes. This alphabet has been developed not through the individual effort of any one type designer, but rather through years of use and modification by many letterers and show-card writers. It comes directly from the practical workbench.

Its proportions vary from narrow letters, such as E, F, and L with their very short crossbars, to round letters, like C and G with their full generous curves.

It is decidedly a fast, freehand brush letter, and a certain amount of character will come with the speed with which this letter is made. Once skill and speed are attained, the letterer will make such personal modifications as he deems fit for the job at hand. The terminals of the letters, for example, may be made either round or square, and this same style may be used with serifs of uniform thickness. For round terminals, flood the brush. To produce square terminals, the brush should be well paletted and worked with the chisel edge.

Even with the addition of new alphabets every few years, this one still remains the show-card writer's single-stroke stand-by, because it is fast, flexible, has character, is ever-modern and extremely legible.

A B C D E F G
H I J K L M N
O P Q R S T U
V W X Y Z

abcdefgh
ijklmnopq
rstuvwxyz

1 2 3 4 5 6 7

8 9 0 ? & ¢

! . , – ( ) ' ; : $

Cartoon or Balloon

THIS style comes to us from the funny page, and has not paused much along the way for any dressing up. It is as sketchy and free-flowing as a well-drawn cartoon. The popularity and widespread use of Cartoon, can easily be explained by the spontaneity which affords a relief from "tight" precision lettering. This sense of relief and its accompanying sense of freedom are welcome to the letterer and to all who look at the lettering.

The cartoon letter is ideal for rush or "knockout" work as it can readily be brushed in in one stroke with either a paletted or a flooded brush, depending upon what kind of terminals are preferred. This alphabet is not limited to the use of the brush, and the letterer can produce speedy and punchy results with a pen.

This informal conversational letter permits the experienced craftsman to ad lib with freedom, as it lends itself to infinite variations. It may be made in italics or straight up and down. Its carefree mood is evident in the crossbars of such letters as A, E, F, etc., which run through and beyond the stems. It dramatically shows the component parts of each letter with disjointed strokes, and makes no attempt at subtle blending or classic order.

It may be used freely on displays, mailing pieces, and posters, but discriminating taste will mark it unfit for austere occasions.

A B C D E F

G H I J K L M

N O P Q R S T

U V W X Y Z

103

a b c d e f

g h i j k l m

n o p q r s t

u v w x y z

1 2 3 4 5 6 7

8 9 0 ? & ¢

$, - , ( ) : , !

Neuland

THE Neuland type designed by Rudolf Koch furnished the model for this brush alphabet. It is strikingly reminiscent of the woodcut technique, revealing the same "accidentals" and ruggedness. The wedge-shaped strokes of unequal width show the imprint of the gouge used in woodcutting, and the unstudied appearance of the letters is typical of tooled work in general.

It may be classified as a block letter alphabet with broken curves, and it may be produced rapidly with lettering brush or pen. Regardless of the tool used, the alphabet should appear rugged and spontaneous. It is not a laborious style, and its irregularities liberate the artist from exacting meticulousness. Neuland is susceptible of innumerable variations, in both form and face. It may be thickened without becoming unduly grotesque.

Although the original type design does not have a lower case, one has here been improvised for hand lettering. The lower case, however, should be used sparingly, as it presents a problem in legibility where it appears in mass copy. The solid black tone of these letters may be lightened by a white or colored inline.

The Neuland letter is a good one for many an advertising or display job which calls for unique treatment. Its rough-hewn masculine strokes can be used not only to symbolize strength and power for industrial subjects, but even for work not directly related to commerce and industry.

ABCDEFG

HIJKLMN

OPQRST

UVWXYZ

107

abcdefgh
jklmnopq
rstuvwxyz

1 2 3 4 5 6 7

8 9 0 ? & $

$. — , ( ) : ' ; !

Gaspipe

THIS is a condensed Gothic alphabet colloquially known as Gaspipe. It is a narrow, single-thick letter with rounded "pipe" corners. Since it is rectangular in form, there are no full curves. It may be made as tall and condensed as you wish, since it derives its charm from an elongated, haughty effect. It should be kept compact and mechanically consistent in width.

It is essentially a reproduction letter requiring the use of ruling pen, T square, and triangle. For careful reproduction work, rule long horizontal pencil guide lines for all crossbars. This will make it possible to maintain uniformity in the position and thickness of the horizontal elements. The center strokes of letters such as B, E, F, G, and H, etc., are all on one level. There is no set rule concerning it, but experience has shown that the Gaspipe alphabet looks best in a light face. If made too heavy and squat, the letters begin to simulate sign painters' characters and lose their classic appeal.

Because of the compactness within the letter itself, it is advisable for the sake of legibility to space these tall letters quite a distance apart. It is rather a simple matter to space this alphabet well, since most of the letters of both upper and lower case fit into a rectangle. This alphabet is one of the most popular current styles, and is used practically everywhere on posters, car cards, billboards, and in magazine advertising. See how many examples of its uses you can find.

A B C D E F

G H I J K L M

O P Q R S T

V W X Y Z

111

a b c d e f g h

i j k l m n o p q

r s t u v w x y z

112

1 2 3 4 5 6 7

8 9 0 ? & ¢

! . , - ( ) ' ; : $

Thick and Thin

THIS is a conservative, sans-serif letter which traces its heritage to the Roman. For freehand work, in order to retain its directness, it should be done with a minimum of brush strokes. Two strokes for the stem and one for the hairline, with small cross strokes to sharpen corners, is a practical procedure to follow. For reproduction purposes, the letter can be made perfect with the use of mechanical instruments.

There is no arbitrary relationship in thickness between the stem and the hairline. It is within the province of the experienced letterer to modify the face of the letter within the limits of propriety. Both capital and small letters are legible even from a distance, and words may be lettered with the upper case alone as well as in combination with the lower case.

This is a perfectly balanced, well-proportioned style that is neither ultramodern nor old-fashioned. For this reason it is just as acceptable in the sheltered sanctum of a library as in the gay lobby of a theater. It is a basic thick-and-thin alphabet which has been used by sign men, show-card and reproduction letterers for years, without becoming a "back number." Like all other basic alphabets designed for service, this one is destined to survive.

A B C D E F

G H I J K L M

N O P Q R S T

U V W X Y Z

a b c d e f g h

i j k l m n o p q

r s t u v w x y z

1 2 3 4 5 6 7

8 9 0 ? & ¢

$. – , O : ; ' !

Thick—and—thin Gaspipe

THIS is a thick-and-thin letter version of the Gaspipe, and its main design theme is the emphasis of the strong vertical and the complete absence of full curves. The vertical scheme is carried through even in letters that ordinarily require diagonal strokes as A, M, W, Y, etc. As in the case of the diagonals in Futura Display on page 155, the diagonals of the V and X are retained here. It was felt that, if the general vertical interpretation were carried through, the V would bear too close a resemblance to the U, and the X might be somewhat confusing.

Like the condensed Gothic, this alphabet is planned on an elongated form. As a matter of fact, the letter can be made any length without appreciably increasing its width. A decided rhythm is created by the repetition of long, strong verticals and delicate horizontals. When the letters are extended in length they are enhanced by a tall and slim appearance; if made wide, the design is spoiled by a squatty distortion.

Because of the fact that most of the letters fit into rectangles of more or less equal width, and because diagonal strokes are few, spacing is comparatively easy. This is just as true of the Futura Bold and the condensed Gaspipe. This entire alphabet can best be made with a ruling pen, since it has a predominance of mechanical verticals that are square to the base. Whether done freehand or for reproduction, this letter is trim looking, modern, and versatile.

A B C D E F

G H I J K L M

N O P Q R S T

U V W X Y Z

119

abcdefg

ijklmnop

rstuvwxyz

120

2 3 4 5 6 7

8 9 0 ? & $

! . , ¬ [ ] ' ; : ¢

Barnum

THIS letter, based on P. T. Barnum and Trapeze type, is a relic of the quaint typography of yesteryear. It has a charm all its own and is an excellent display letter that seems to blend the present with the past. The preeminent characteristic—thin stems combined with weighted top and bottom horizontals, and equally heavy serifs—makes Barnum a letter easily discernible and easily remembered. This quality runs through the entire alphabet in upper and lower case, signs, and numerals.

The predominance of straight lines prompts the use of the ruling pen as an aid to exact rendering. Where the nature of the job does not warrant absolute exactness, Barnum may be done with a brush, employing the build-up technique.

Surprising as it may seem, the Barnum style, as gay as a minstrel song, is not limited to circus banners, or to wild West notices of "Reward—Dead or Alive." It fits in just as graciously on art exhibition announcements, and on dignified posters advertising a ball at the Ritz.

This letter, therefore, may be said to owe its revived popularity to its versatility, its quaintness, and its simplicity of construction.

A B C D E F
G H I J K L M
N O P Q R S T
U V W X Y Z

123

abcdefgh

ijklmnopq

rstuvwxyz

1 2 3 4 5 6 7

8 9 0 ? & $

. , - [ ] ' ; : ¢

Gothic Display

THIS is an elephantine, powerful Gothic with the top and bottom of each letter flattened so that it will be flush with the guide lines. This treatment is evident in the C, G, J, K, S, etc. Most of the letters seem to fit into, and pretty well occupy, the confines of a square. This alphabet has stocky, abbreviated ascenders and descenders which help carry out the general squatty effect. The semblance of a serif on the A is an interesting appendage to this sans-serif alphabet.

A line of this lettering appears as a solid black block, with the white areas within the letters giving texture to the mass. The horizontals of the capitals have been made slightly thinner than the stems. This liberty has been taken for the purpose of increasing legibility by permitting more white space to show within the letter. This same scheme is carried through wherever necessary in the lower case and numerals. Another way of relieving the blackness is to introduce a white or colored center inline within each letter.

Gothic Display, a bold, heavy-duty letter of strong poster value, is fine for travel displays, theatrical banners, and other work where strength and sheer boldness play an important part in forceful advertising.

A B C D E F

G H I J K L M

N O P Q R S

T U V W X Y Z

127

a b c d e f

g h i j k l m

n o p q r s t

u v w x y z

128

1 2 3 4 5 6 7

8 9 0 ? & ¢

$. – , ( ) : ; !

Cooper

HERE is a posterized Roman alphabet that comes highly endorsed. It is based on the type design by Oswald Cooper, and is noted for the following characteristics:

The serifs, bluntly round and padded, are integral parts of the letter. Variations in the serifs will not lessen the vitality of the letter forms. The curved stems, together with the chubby serifs, remove any semblance of mechanical precision from these characters. The letters in general are of a flowing, liquid type where every single part of the letter blends into the other parts. This gives a pleasant, well-knit effect to words and groups of words.

This is a built-up letter and is best made with the chisel side of a fully-charged brush. Bold, rapid strokes should be used. Precision instruments should by all means be avoided. In planning to use this alphabet, one may choose to make it light face, bold face, or even black face. Different effects will naturally result from these gradations of tone. In any case, the letters should be made so close together that one letter should almost touch its neighbor.

Enough variations of these characters may be conceived by a lettering artist with an eye toward creative design to satisfy even the most rebellious dissenter who complains about the general rigidity of lettering styles.

ABCDEF

GHIJKLM

NOPQRST

UVWXYZ

131

a b c d e f
g h i j k l m
n o p q r s t
u v w x y z

1 2 3 4 5 6 7

8 9 0 ? & ¢

$. — , [ ] : ' ; !

Roman

THE capitals of the Roman alphabet as revealed by the impeccable inscription on the base of the Trajan Column represent the original source of our modern letter forms.

The alphabet shown here is a brush version which may be rendered single-stroke or in the build-up technique. Some say that the Roman alphabet is as unchangeable as the human anatomy. This is an inspired though somewhat fanatical attitude. The Roman, most legible of all letter forms, is not a rigid, inflexible alphabet; it is subject to countless variations. For example, the exact forms of the serifs and swashes is largely a matter of personal taste; the weight or swell of the curves may be in the center of the letter or at an angle; and the terminus of the J may rest on the base line or extend below it. It shows slight modulation in the hairlines which add character to the letters. The slightly curved serifs are blended into the stems by means of soft, bracketed fillets.

It might perhaps be well even for a professional letterer of long experience occasionally to refer to and study the ancient original of this classic alphabet, sans adulterations. In this way he will revive his initial inspiration and counteract the effects of the detours he has naturally made by his continual modifications of the original. The Roman alphabet, a perennial favorite, offers us a choice letter for all phases of sedate advertising. It is a time-honored, venerable alphabet revered alike by letterer and layman.

A B C D E F
G H I J K L M
N O P Q R S T
U V W X Y Z

135

a b c d e f g h
i j k l m n o p q
r s t u v w x y z

1 2 3 4 5 6 7

8 9 0 ? & ¢

$. - , ( ) : ; !

Futura Condensed

THE Futura alphabet, known to some perhaps as Egyptian, may be made condensed or extended to suit space limitations or to create a definite impression. In essence, the Futura is a one-thickness, sans-serif Gothic, and one of the most legibile alphabets ever devised. It may be made equally well with brush or pen.

It is a letter of bare essentials, completely purged of artificial embellishments, and for this reason some teachers of lettering start the student with this alphabet. This plan is not recommended here. Instead, the student is urged to acquire his initial lettering experience from the more elementary single-thick, single-stroke alphabet shown on page 99.

The Futura condensed is too difficult to be executed in the one-stroke technique by the beginner; it must be done cautiously. It is more difficult than it looks. Even an experienced letterer, if he rushes it, may find that he has to true it up for finished sharpness. It may be done freehand or for careful reproduction work, with the aid of instruments. For fine work it might be advisable, where the layout permits it, to use the Futura extended, with its perfect circles playing an important part in the letter form, thus making it possible to use compasses.

The fine restraint of these letters depicts the structural and functional mood of our time. Futura is not just a fad alphabet, but rather an entirely practical style that has made a permanent place for itself in the field of lettering.

A B C D E F

G H I J K L M

N O P Q R S T

U V W X Y Z

139

a b c d e f g h
i j k l m n o p q r
s t u v w x y z

1 2 3 4 5 6 7

8 9 0 ? & ¢

$. - , ( ) : ' ; !

Broadway

THIS recently modernized alphabet is a distant cousin of the old-time Broadway type. Its general combination of thick and thin strokes may be said to reflect the spirit of Beauty and the Beast. The extremely heavy stems give stamina and power; a strength that is happily tempered with grace and delicacy. Note the slight curve or waist line of the stems, and the slightly accented hairlines.

Whereas the original inspiration for this alphabet did not have a lower case, this adapted version can boast of a "full house"—upper and lower case, numerals, and signs. The lower case is not so often used as the upper because it cannot claim great legibility. At a distance, one is conscious only of the rhythmic beat of stocky blocks of black, interspersed with thin strokes. This chic alphabet has its place on program covers, posters to be viewed at close range, and artistic displays where design holds precedence over readability.

When producing these letters, the stems are built up, and the graceful hairlines are made with a single stroke. Use the same brush for the hairlines, for the stems, and for "squaring off" top and bottom terminals. For reproduction work, straight lines may be substituted for the subtle curves in the stems so as to permit the use of a ruling pen.

This alphabet is, on the whole, more of a display letter than a text letter, but it is withal a welcome addition to the letterer's repertory.

A B C D E F

G H I J K L M

N O P Q R S T

U V W X Y Z

143

abcdefghi
jklmnopq
rstuvwxyz

1234567

890?&¢

$.-,():;!

Diploma

THE Diploma alphabet is closely related to the reed writing of antiquity, and is executed with either a brush or a broad-nibbed pen. It may be made single-stroke or as a built-up letter. If the single-stroke technique is used, stroke the brush well on the palette in order to secure a good flat chisel edge. To get the fine modulation of line from a hairline to a heavy stroke, do not twirl the brush between the fingers —even around curves. For the hairlines, use the side of the chisel in much the same fashion as you would use the side of a flat pen. For the build-up technique, use a brush large enough to enable you to make the heavy elements with no more than two strokes. Use a fine pen or small pointed brush for extra-fine endings and embellishments.

This alphabet is used for diplomas, charters, religious documents, greeting cards, slogans and mottoes, occasionally for poetry, and wherever an academic impression is to be conveyed. The capital letters of this alphabet are not used alone to form words; they are used in combination with the lower case.

The Diploma, as well as other text alphabets, allows considerable freedom and latitude for modification, as there are no rigidly fixed patterns for the characters. The thing to remember is to get free-flowing curves with a natural play of thick and thin strokes. The Diploma style is similar to Old English except that it is simpler, more legible, and consequently more practical.

146

A B C D E F
G H I J K L M
N O P Q R S T
U V W X Y Z

147

a b c d e f g h
i j k l m n o p q
r s t u v w x y z

1 2 3 4 5 6 7

8 9 0 ? & ¢

§ . - , ( ) : ; !

Old English

EVERY letterer should acquaint himself with at least one of the text alphabets commonly known as Old English. Originally made with the single strokes of a reed pen, today it is made with pen or brush, but is still found more applicable to penwork.

The use of the Old English alphabet is not widespread in America. Its aristocratic and pedantic appearance reserves it for religious writings, legends for Biblical scenes, and wherever there are effects calling for the historical, the antique, and the quaint. The capitals of this alphabet should be used only for the beginning of a word, but never for spelling out the entire word.

It can safely be said that no other style of lettering permits as much liberty with scrolls and flourishes as the Old English. As a matter of fact, hardly two letterers can be found to agree in every respect upon a fixed pattern for making these letters. There is mutual agreement only on the spirit and general effect, not on the details of each letter. The accompanying plate shows a variation of Old English that is less complicated than most others. It has shed many of the entangling hairlines and extravagant flourishes, and the resulting simplification makes it more practical for the letterer and more legible for the reader.

If compared with the Diploma alphabet on page 147, Old English is found to be more angular and less legible. The embellishments of both these alphabets may be further enhanced by illumination and ornamentation within the letter.

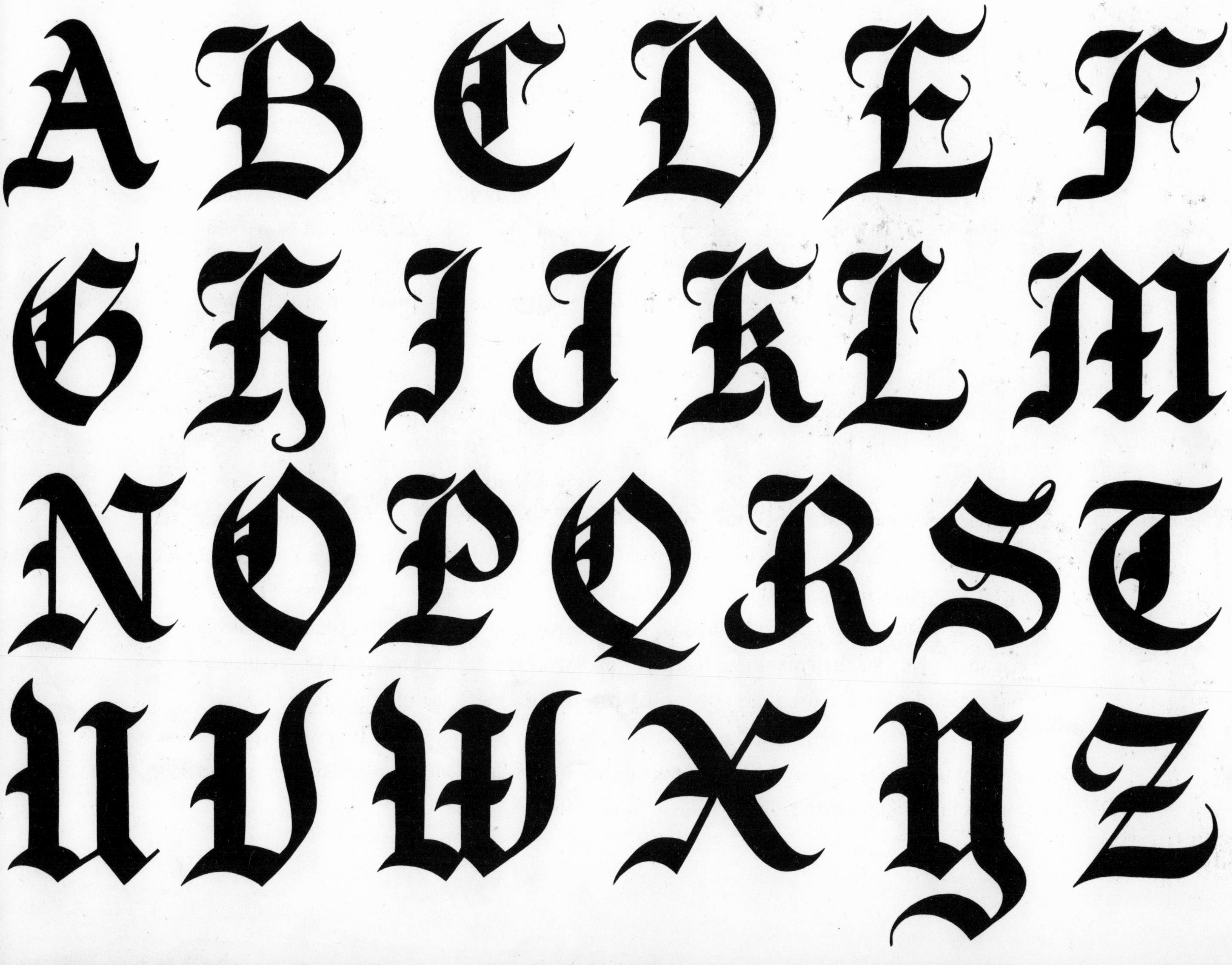

A B C D E F
G H I J K L M
N O P Q R S T
U V W X Y Z

151

abcdefgh
ijklmnopq
rstuvwxyz

152

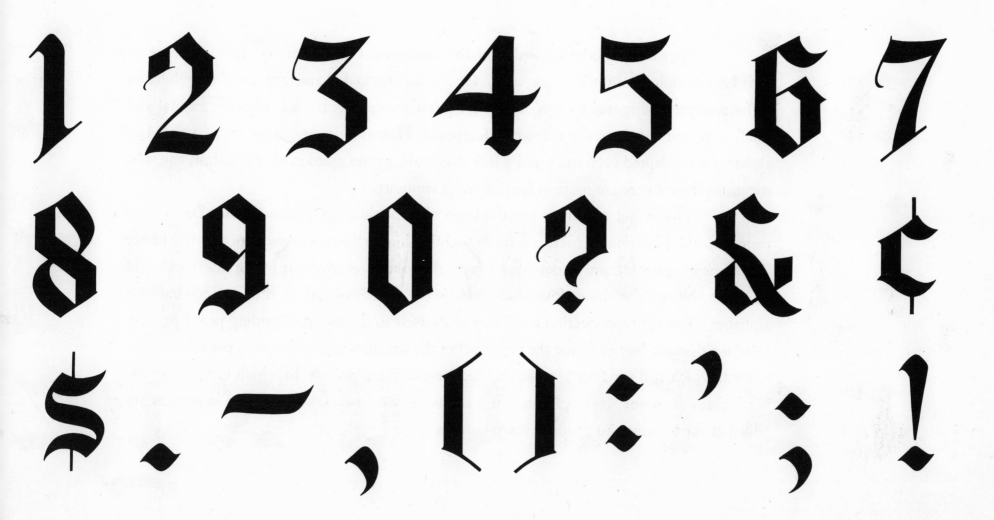

153

Futura Display

HERE is a modern alphabet of the condensed Gothic variety. It is a relative of the Gaspipe alphabet shown on page 119. One of the marked characteristics of this alphabet is the absence of diagonal strokes. There are a few exceptions to this, as in the capital and small v, x, and z, where the diagonals do appear. However, in the type from which this alphabet was adapted even the v and x lack diagonals. In the opinion of the author, the substitutions shown here are more in keeping with legibility.

This is not strictly a one-thickness alphabet and, as in the Gothic Display on page 127, the horizontal strokes are made slightly thinner to relieve some of the blackness. The same design structure of condensed vertical strokes is carried out in the lower case and numerals. Notice the almost humorous twist in the swash, or tail, of the Q. This built-up alphabet is fine for reproduction work as it lends itself to the use of the ruling pen. For free-hand brushwork, however, use the flat chisel of the brush, well stroked on a palette. Choose a brush which will produce a stroke the thickness of the crossbars. In which case, the crossbar is made with one stroke, the stem is made with two strokes, and short cross strokes are added at the terminals to produce sharp corners.

A B C D E F

G H I J K L M

O P Q R S T

V W X Y Z

155

a b c d e f g h i

j k l m n o p q

r s t u v w x y z

156

1 2 3 4 5 6 7

8 9 0 ? & ¢

$. — , ( ) ; ' : !

Futura Black

THIS plate shows one of the ultramodern alphabets in the advanced school of lettering design. The general visual impression that it gives is that of a black mass with a thin white strip laid over it.

This alphabet has been so designed and modified as to be stripped of all incidentals, including crossbars in the A and H. The reader's imagination is given the opportunity to fill in the connecting links and thus complete the picture. In other words, the designer of the type, Paul Renner, has concerned himself more with pure design than with orthodox rendering.

As a result, legibility with this popular style becomes the concern of the letterer and his layout. He should leave plenty of white space around words and between lines, so that these heavy letters will not appear to be meaningless blotches of black color. The corners of the stems should be sharp and square. One should not use this alphabet on a rush job, since to rush it is to ruin it. It is a specialty style suitable for use wherever an "eye-catcher" is required, and yet it is not blatant. Its real charm and appeal lie in its substantial, precise appearance and stark simplification of the letter form.

This alphabet is best adapted to isolated headings, spot lettering, letterheads, labels, and wherever one desires or dares to inject a note of modernism.

ABCDEF
GHIJKLM
NOPQRST
UVWXYZ

159

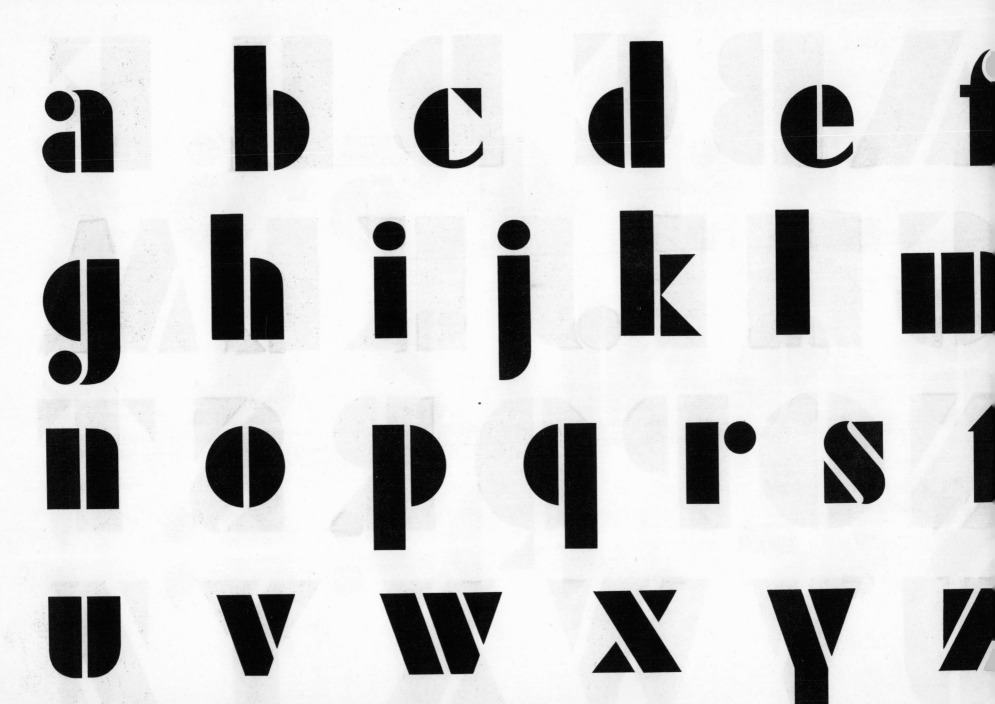

2 3 4 5 6 7

8 9 0 ? & ¢

$. - , () : ; !

Kabel

KABEL is a flawless type, designed by Rudolf Koch, which glorifies the use of mechanical instruments. It is a modernized Gothic reproduction letter whose form is based on the circle and the straight line. It deviates but little from this mold, and remains rather formal and precise looking. This alphabet is remarkable for its even tone, its dignity and precision.

The original Kabel type shows the influence of mechanical instruments even in the S. In the version shown here, the upper and lower case S were both made freehand and appear less stilted than the original type. To do full justice to this alphabet requires the use of the ruling pen and compasses, but the purity of its style and balance need not be impaired when the letter is modified for brushwork. For rapid work, Kabel should be made with single strokes. Perhaps a little touch just here and there to sharpen up corners, and to give the alphabet the clean-cut effect that distinguishes it, would not be amiss. The terminals may be either oblique or square.

This is one of the finest alphabets a letterer can use, since it is seldom out of place, however exclusive its surroundings may be. For a feminine motif, Kabel can be made in a lighter face, retaining the same structural characteristics. For perfect symmetry, balanced **proportion**, and inherent beauty, Kabel **cannot** easily be surpassed.

A B C D E F
G H I J K L M
N O P Q R S T
U V W X Y Z

163

abcdefgh
ijklmnopq
rstuvwxyz

164

1 2 3 4 5 6 7

8 9 0 ? & ¢

$. — , ( ) : ' ; !

165

Fine Gothic Moderne

HERE is a well-designed, distinguished-looking alphabet that has no exact counterpart in printer's type. It is an easy letter to remember and recognize, because of its exaggerated proportions, its fullness of curves, and the interesting position of its crossbars. It is shown here in light face, with all strokes thin and uniform, since it appears to best advantage this way.

This modern Gothic is essentially a reproduction letter and its round, smooth-flowing curves yield themselves to the exactness of compass and ruling pen. Its graceful proportions (subject to discreet modifications), appeal strongly to refined taste. Because of its light face it should not be burdened with a long message of text. It is happily used where it need only convey an impression, rather than deliver a specific message. This alphabet is widely used on letterheads, book-jackets, package designs, magazine covers, and labels. Its modern dignified bearing lends "class" to any product with which it is associated.

If done freehand for ordinary show-card work, it should be made single-stroke with a well-charged brush. For rounded terminals and even strokes, work with the tip of the flooded brush, and barely press down upon the paper. Naturally, the brush technique can only begin to approach the effect possible with mechanical tools. But, although the round letters will be optically rather than mechanically round, much character can be put into the brush version of this alphabet.

A B C D E F
G H I J K L M
N O P Q R S T
U V W X Y Z

167

a b c d e f g h
i j k l m n o p q
r s t u v w x y z

168

1 2 3 4 5 6 7

8 9 0 & ? $

! . , — ( ) : ; ¢

Eve

This delicate Roman alphabet is distinguished by its serifs and tapering strokes. The letters are of varying widths. The C, D, G, O, and Q show great rotundity; the A is exceptionally wide; the B, P, S, and T are especially narrow. This variation creates pleasing rhythm and balance when the letters are used in words and groups of words.

A study of this alphabet will reveal a number of surprising but pleasant inconsistencies in the structure of some of its letters. For example, the S is sans-serif; there is a vigorous diagonal in the Y, which extends below the guide line; accented diagonal strokes in the M, N, V, W, and X do not taper; and the heavy horizontal strokes of the Z are connected by a thin diagonal. Modifications are possible in most of the letters, and in the lower case it is especially tempting to experiment with such characters as the a, e, g, and k. The g shown in the lower-case plate has been considerably altered from the type, without forfeiting the spirit of the letter form.

Owing to the delicacy of its construction, Eve should be used in a fitting background. It is a fine reproduction letter combining copperplate finesse with a certain amount of freedom, and it should not be made to hobnob with a mixed society of letters, but should be reserved for the "finer things in life."

ABCDEF
GHIJKLM
NOPQRST
UVWXYZ

171

abcdefgh
ijklmnopq
rstuvwxyz

1 2 3 4 5 6 7

8 9 0 ? & ¢

! . , – ( ) : ; $

Italics

ITALICIZED words are used to denote emphasis and to give the effect of speed. Straight up-and-down alphabets may be italicized by tipping the letters at a slant. The degree of the slant is largely a matter of judgment, but the slant should not be so steep as to make reading difficult.

Some people find it easier to do italics than upright lettering. The slanted letter, akin to the tilt of ordinary handwriting, can be made more rapidly than straight up-and-down lettering. In vertical letters, it may be added, any deviation from squareness shows up more than a deviation from a given angle in slanted letters. In other words, even an untrained eye can note letters that fall over when they are supposed to be upright. It requires a discerning eye, on the other hand, to detect any slight differences in the degree of the angle in italicized letters.

The italic shown here is a slanted version of the Roman alphabet. This is more evident in the upper case than in the lower case. The capital letters, if stood up straight, would immediately be identified as Roman letters. The a, f, j, y, etc., of the lower case show a definite cursive quality—a departure from the upright Roman alphabet.

The italic is a popular alphabet for show-cards as well as for reproduction work.

A B C D E F

G H I J K L M

N O P Q R S T

U V W X Y Z

175

abcdefgh

ijklmnopq

rstuvwxyz

176

1 2 3 4 5 6 7

8 9 0 ? & ¢

$. - , ( ) : ' ; !

Swash Capitals

THE decorative capitals shown here do not owe allegiance to any particular printer's type. When analyzed, they are found to be freely designed italics with dynamic swash flourishes. This is a thick-and-thin letter with a rather daring slant, and its character is crystallized in its fleshy serifs and terminals. The weight or swell of the curves is not in the center, but on a diagonal plane (as is obvious in the O). This alphabet is reminiscent of the heading used on the *Saturday Evening Post* magazine cover.

The swash italic may be used as a decorative initial for monograms, for the beginnings of words, and occasionally for complete words.

ABCDEF

GHIJKLM

NOP2RST

UVWXYZ

179

Kaufmann

THIS uniformly thick, ribbonlike script, perpetuated in the type of M. R. Kaufmann, is effective on displays and posters and is frequently used in reproduction work. It is legible at a distance as well as at close range.

The links which connect the letters to form words and simulate orderly handwriting are of the same thickness as the letters, and all the characters are at a similarly fixed slant—thus creating a pleasing rhythm. The letters may be made to slant, as shown in the accompanying plates, or they may be made erect and perpendicular to the guide line. The terminals of the strokes may be either square or round. In the lower case, it should be noted, the outer curves of the connecting links are round, whereas the inside ones are sharp. As a rule, the upward joining stroke is added to the last letter of each word to carry through the rhythmic pattern.

The highly personalized upper case offers many temptations for modification. Each letterer can use his own handwriting as an aid to injecting a personal touch in the design of the capitals. The lower case, on the other hand, is more standardized. Words should not be formed with the capital letters alone, as they are not legible in continuous reading matter. These should be reserved for initials.

$$a\ B\ C\ D\ E\ F$$

$$G\ H\ J\ J\ K\ L\ M$$

$$N\ O\ P\ 2\ R\ S\ T$$

$$U\ V\ W\ X\ Y\ Z$$

181

abcdefgh
ijklmnopq
rstuvwxyz

182

1 2 3 4 5 6 7

8 9 0 ? & ¢

$. - , ( ) ; ' : !

183

Trafton

THIS is a cursive letter embodying all the beauty of fine calligraphy. Its sweeping curves show an interesting interplay of thick and thin strokes, and it may be done single-stroke with a brush or a flat-nibbed pen.

The dynamic loops of letters such as B, H, P, etc., extend beyond the guide lines with a daring lack of restraint. The lower case, numerals, and signs reflect the cheerful spirit of a good penman. This is exhibited by the long descenders and ascenders, the delightful twists and turns of many of the loops, and the oversized dots of the i and j. The ampersand is an excellent example of the same spirit of animation. The capitals can be used for isolated initials, for the beginning of words, paragraphs, and chapters. When writing words, they should be combined with the more conservative and formal lower case.

This alphabet should be closely spaced and may be made either in the form of an italic, that is, without the letters touching, or as a script with the letters joined. It is a display letter suitable for work of refinement and delicacy. Unlike the Kaufmann script shown on page 181, the Trafton is not easily read at a distance and should, therefore, be reserved for work read at close range.

The designer of the type, Howard A. Trafton, is to be lauded for this typographical creation which combines a sensitive taste with a playful spirit.

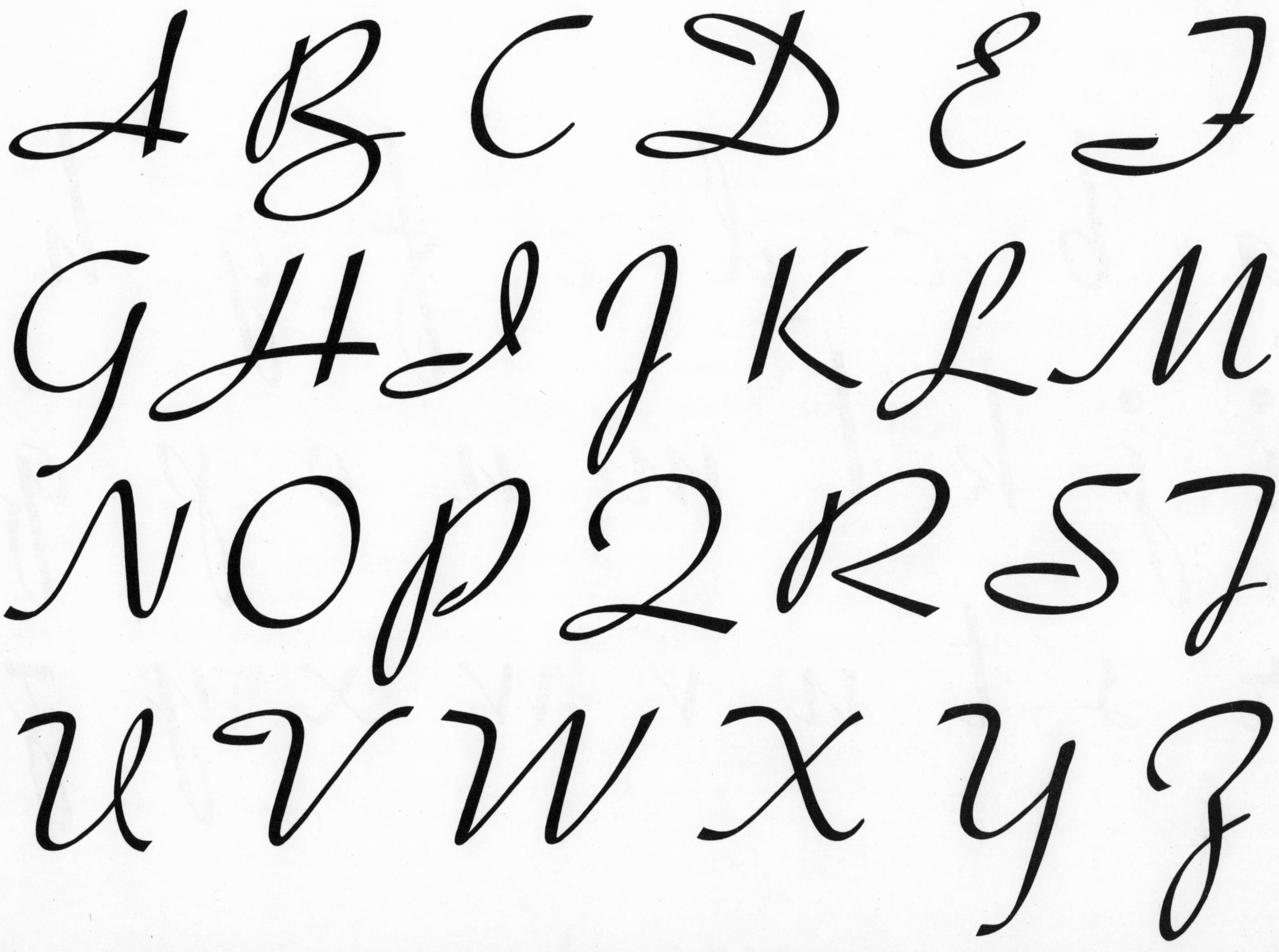

A B C D E F
G H I J K L M
N O P Q R S T
U V W X Y Z

185

a b c d e f g h
i j k l m n o p q
r s t u v w x y z

1 2 3 4 5 6 7

8 9 0 ? & ¢

$. - , ( ) : ; ; !

Legend

LEGEND, designed by F. H. Ernst Schneidler, shows the influence of the medieval scribe and his reed pen. It is fine for penwork, and may also be done in the single-stroke brush technique. It is a free, unrestrained letter, and something of a calligraphic enigma. The more you study its characteristics the more surprised you will be to find that it defies analysis and seems to revel in delightful inconsistencies. The great difference in thickness between hairline and stem, owing to the natural flexibility of the lettering tool, lends vigor to this strange alphabet.

In the capital letters, the B seems to possess much more dynamic vitality than the more conservative U. The sudden surging curve of the D, the vigorous diagonal of the M, and the surprising upward swash of the Y—all take the reader unawares and leave him breathless. In the lower case, there are countless differences in the slants and angles of the letters. In the main, this alphabet may be said to strive for effect and force, and not for cold consistency. Do not judge it from ordinary standards of preciseness—it belongs in a class by itself. It represents a radical departure from the run-of-the-mill styles.

Since it is so unpredictable, and shows such a luxurious lack of restraint, Legend should be used only after careful consideration. It adds a unique touch to individualized spot lettering, on posters, titles, and chapter headings for certain types of books and magazines. You will recognize it as the alphabet style used for the chapter headings of this book.

A B C D E F
G H I J K L M
N O P Q R S T
U V W X Y Z

189

a b c d e f g h
i j k l m n o p q
r s t u v w x y z

190

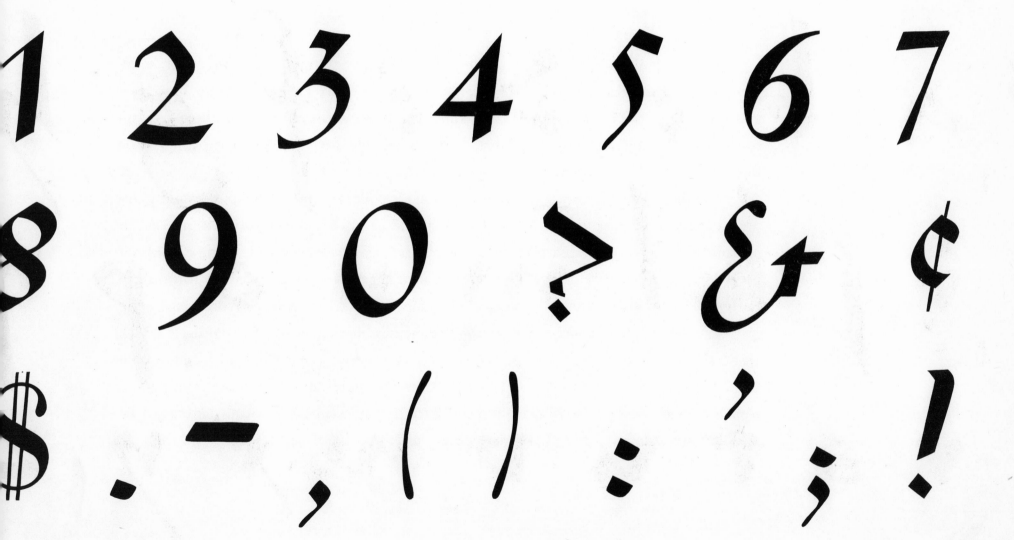

Beton

THE alphabet shown on the opposite page, an extremely beautiful letter, is referred to by printers as Beton Open Face, and was designed by Heinrich Jost in 1930. It is really a form of thick-and-thin Roman with sharp, square serifs. There is nothing freakish or particularly new about this alphabet. It has been used for years by sign painters in a modified way, and is now enjoying a popular revival.

Beton is definitely a formal letter which it is almost impossible, and certainly impracticable to do freehand. For best results, it should be made mechanically with the aid of instruments. However, it is a time-consuming letter, and when the lack of time does not permit the necessary care it should be made solid rather than in outline. In this form it can easily be made with a brush. When made solid, the shadow effect is usually dispensed with.

Since this alphabet is highly effective for headings and spot catchwords, it is well worth the trouble to take pains to do it carefully. When well done, it is ideal for illustrated catalogue work and for descriptive headings in artistic publications. A lower case to this alphabet would be too complicated and too infrequently used by the hand letterer to be included in this series of practical hand-lettering plates.

A B C D E F
G H I J K L M
N O P Q R S T
U V W X Y Z

193

Individualized Capitals

THE accompanying plate presents capital letter forms which can be evolved from one's own handwriting. The letters may be made straight up and down or tilted forward or backward, but a certain degree of consistency should govern this new-found freedom. To posterize your handwriting successfully requires an appreciation of the inherent beauty of calligraphy, as well as seasoned lettering experience.

In this plate the author's own handwriting has been treated from the point of view of lettering design, and brings to the fore the outstanding advantages of such an alphabet used in advertising. The letters seem personal and intimate, and they appear free from meticulous labor. There is no lettering style which can show more originality, exclusiveness, and that "custom-made" quality. For, after all, no two people will show the same cursive traits. For that matter, even the same letterer will not consistently produce identical forms. Just as in any form of artistic expression, one's mood at the time directly influences the creative manifestations.

A pretty handwriting is not the great desideratum for this posterization. A vigorous handwriting, revealing character, is far more desirable as a basis for improvisation. The actual procedure in interpreting your script is outlined on page 196. It is hoped that the reader, having been shown the way, will be encouraged to modify his individualized script to lend charm and spontaneity to initials and monograms.

194

A B C D E F

G H I J K L M

N O P Q R S T

U V W X Y Z

195

Individualized Script

You can use your own handwriting as a basis for creating an individualized lettering script. The procedure, as illustrated in the accompanying plate, is outlined as follows:

1. *Write*

   On several slips of paper, write your copy a few time as naturally and rapidly as possible. If your natural handwriting has too regular a form, or if it is of the "pretty" species, experiment with slanting the letters a new way or changing the pressure on your pencil. From the several specimens you have made, select that one which best brings out the mood or character you wish to represent.

2. *Posterize*

   With the selected specimen as a model, make a rough posterized lettering sketch of the copy, following the same essential character. Do this in pencil, and give body to the letters by building them up to double thickness.

3. *Outline*

   Trace or copy the sketchy lines of the posterized version of your handwriting, making desirable modifications. Work this over until you have a sharp, clean, finished outline.

4. *Paint in*

   Paint or ink in the lettering smoothly with brush or pen. If necessary, touch up with opaque white. Individualized script will find a ready place on trade-marks, labels, and permanent industrial signatures.

1. *Manfredi*

2. *Manfredi*

3. *Manfredi*

4. *ORIGINAL Manfredi DISPLAYS*

197

Effect Lettering

EFFECT, or picturized, lettering has always held a fascination for those with a dramatic turn of mind. It is a form of stylized picture writing, representing a definite concept.

The accompanying plate by no means attempts to fix standard patterns for representing stock ideas. It is merely suggestive of common styles and techniques used to interpret idea words such as "hot" and "cold." The particular method of rendering, and the tool and medium used, will depend upon the nature of the design at hand. As stated before, this plate does not show the entire gamut of effects, practically every dramatic thought can be exemplified in lettering, and interpretations will vary with the experience and imagination of the letterer. A good letterer with a fertile imagination will find it an exciting adventure to devise new lettering forms to dramatize "thin," "thick," "shadow," "play," "burst," "rope," "grizzly," "glitter," and many others. For unusual effects, experiment with broad, soft, chisel-edged pencils. This will produce a ribbonlike quality and create a nice interplay of thick and thin strokes.

Effect lettering is found extremely adaptable for theatrical work and for "spot" lettering in all forms of graphic art advertising. It is important to remember to use effect lettering with restraint. Do not damage the effect of effect lettering by showing too much of it on one card.

HOT

ORIENT

COLD

RADIO

Ribbon

FEAR

POWER

SPEED

RUSTIC

199

Layouts

HERE is a fascinating game-study that is highly instructive in the principles of layout. Cutting colored paper into geometric forms, such as circles, squares, rectangles, and triangles of various proportions, and pasting these cutouts onto a background provides a worth-while art experience.

Using a card of about 5″ x 7″ as a background, plan an interesting layout for the project at hand. Each cutout form represents an integral part of the whole composition; it may be part of the lettering or of the design. Manipulate these elementary forms about the card, trying out different relationships. You will find that a good layout "satisfies," while a poor one "annoys." Create a number of layouts and see which ones are satisfiers and which are annoyers. A satisfying layout shows fine proportion, rhythmic relationship, interesting contrast in color and mass, and harmony within variety.

When you have hit upon a satisfying layout, affix the paper forms to the background with rubber cement. If some details are too fine to be cut out of paper, supplement the paste-up with a little hand decoration.

The accompanying plate presents the results of a project by a student at the School of Industrial Art. For these layouts the student was limited to two colors and white. For practical use, many colors may be employed, thus providing a preview, in full color, of the proposed poster.

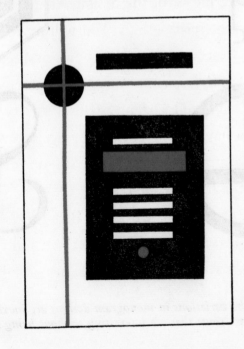

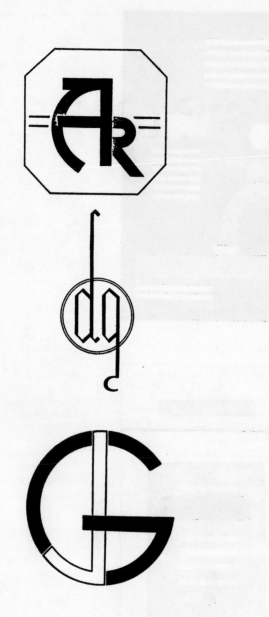

The variations in monogram designs are inexhaustible.
Here are some that are interesting without being too involved.

Shop Hints and Safety Precautions

CHAPTER 9

FOR BRUSHES—A good letterer takes special pride in the selection and care of his brushes. He forms an almost sentimental attachment for them and is inspired to keep them in serviceable condition for many years.

Selection of Brushes.

1. A good brush, the letterer's silent partner, will respond readily to his slightest touch.

2. The hairs of a good brush are of uniform length, and are perfectly straight. Inferior brushes may be recognized by their kinky hairs of unequal length.

3. Show-card brushes may be classified according to the *length* of hair:

   (*a*) Short—   Does not hold much paint. Is best used for short-stroke letters.

   (*b*) Medium—Is good for general work. If only one brush can be afforded, a medium-length one is recommended.

   (*c*) Long—   Is good for built-up letters, for certain types of reproduction work, for painting borders and outlining lettering.

4. Professional letterers do not use a small brush where a large one is required. Unnecessary strokes waste time.

5. Where more than one color is used on a job, a separate brush should be devoted to each color. Too frequent cleaning of the brush while working means wasted effort and loss of time.

Care of Brushes.

1. Where short curly hairs appear out of alignment, pull out entire hair length with the aid of a pair of tweezers.

2. It is advisable to rinse the brush occasionally while working, to keep the heel free from caked-up paint.

3. Show-card brush hairs become passive and lifeless from use with glue, and oil colors. These brushes should be restricted to lettering with show-card color.

4. Use cold water for washing the brush after use. Hot water will dissolve the setting compound which holds the hair within the ferrule.

5. After washing, water should be gently shaken out of brush hair, or stroked with a soft rag.

6. For carrying brushes on your person, a narrow case or bag is ideal. This container should be long enough not to cramp the hair. It should be so held that the brushes will stand on the handle, not on the hair.

7. Brushes may be stored for a long time by standing them in a glass jar or vase with hair side up and handle side down. Sprinkle camphor or moth balls in the container before you close it, to preserve the hair from moths.

FOR COLORS

1. Poster colors may be thinned when necessary by the addition of ordinary water.

2. When thinning paint, stir entire contents thoroughly, so as not to leave any lumps at the bottom of the jar.

3. Certain colors, like emerald green, cerise, mauve, and turquoise blue, contain aniline dye and will "bleed" through and discolor any white poster color painted over them. They should not be used for backgrounds on which white lettering is to appear. If such a background is unavoidable, use Japan white thinned with turpentine for the lettering.

4. When working with the paint, take out a little and spread it on a palette, instead of dipping your brush into the jar each time.

5. Keep paint jar cover clean, inside and out.

6. Keep spiral rim of glass jar free from paint. This affords airtight protection and facility in opening.

7. Keep jar well closed when not in use, to prevent evaporation and caking of color.

8. Constant "reviving" of dried-up color with water will cause the color to "dust off" when dry. To redeem this color, add some glue or mucilage to act as a binder.

9. It is not generally wise to experiment with making or doctoring colors.

FOR INDIA INK

1. To coat in large areas with India ink, use a large soft brush. This gives a solid, even coat and prevents streakiness.

2. Poster color can be applied over an area painted in with India ink. The color (even if it is white) will retain its value. India ink is waterproof when dry, and does not bleed through. Lettering or design done with India ink over an area painted with poster color will crack and peel off.

FOR PENCILS

1. Keep pencil lead away from lips.

2. Hard-leaded, long-pointed pencils should not be kept in open pockets. They are a menace to safety.

3. If you use a knife or razor blade for sharpening, hold the pencil firmly in position so that the sharpening movements are directed *away* from the body.

FOR RUBBER CEMENT

1. A patented glass dispenser equipped with an adjustable brush and a convenient cover provides the best means of keeping rubber cement ready for use.

2. For best adhesion, the card or paper to be pasted, as well as the surface upon which it is to be applied, should both be brushed or scraped in with the cement.

3. Rubber cement is volatile and should be kept covered.

4. Rubber cement is highly inflammable and should be kept away from excessive heat.

5. Dried-up rubber cement accumulated around the container may be salvaged. Kneaded and rolled into a ball, it makes an excellent eraser.

FOR STORING IMPLEMENTS

1. T squares, drawing boards, celluloid triangles, and rulers should be kept away from moisture and heat to prevent warpage. Provide a regular place to hang or store them so that they will be within reach when needed and out of the way when not in use.

FOR PAPER CUTTER

1. When using the cutter, always get a good firm grip on the blade handle.

2. The handle should be raised and brought down to position for a complete cut. Suspending the handle in mid-air may allow it to fall unexpectedly and cause serious injury.

3. Reserve the cutter for paper and cardboard. Cutting metal or nails will nick the blade.

FOR INSTRUMENT SET

1. Keep set away from edge of table, where instruments are likely to be brushed to the floor.

2. An instrument, nicked or mutilated in any way, cannot be used in that condition for

precise work. Dulled or injured blades require resharpening by patient, even stroking on a whetstone.

3. When not in use, store the set in a closed case. This prevents the loss of small parts and retards oxidation of the metal.

MISCELLANEOUS

1. It is perverted economy to make your own brushes, tools, or paints, for professional equipment is better and more economical in the long run.

2. Keep the table cleared of unnecessary paraphernalia. Crowding hampers free movement and may lead to smearing or spilling of paint or water.

3. The following sentences, each of which contains every letter of the alphabet, are ideal for practice work:

   (*a*) The quick brown fox jumps over a lazy dog.

   (*b*) Pack my box with five dozen liquor jugs.

SILK SCREEN PRINTING PROCESS

For those who are called upon to produce identical posters in quantity, the silk screen stencil process of reproduction is highly recommended. It is an inexpensive way of duplicating lettering and designs in any quantity and size, and in any number of colors. The use of this process will mean a tremendous saving in time and money. With one stencil as many as four hundred cards may be printed in one hour, and the stencil will last indefinitely. What is more, the reproduced posters will compare favorably with the hand-lettered original. The small studio equipment entails a negligible initial and maintenance expenditure and takes up little room.

For a full understanding of the simple methods employed in this unique process, the reader is referred to the author's *Silk Screen Stencil Craft as a Hobby*, published by Harper & Brothers. This reading may be supplemented by the *Silk Screen Printing Process* by Biegeleisen and Busenbark, published by the McGraw-Hill Book Company, which covers a more thorough treatment of the subject for professional needs.

Selling Your Lettering

CHAPTER 10

THOSE who have diligently advanced thus far along the progressive stages of learning to letter have now reached a point where they may pause and take stock. They have attained a summit where they may relax from practice and exercises and extend their energies and thoughts in a new direction.

The serious student will concentrate on ways and means of capitalizing on his newly acquired skill. He will try to determine into which niche of the lettering field he fits best. When he has decided this, he will commence to plan the self-selling campaign that is preliminary to his being accepted into that niche.

Finding a position is in most instances dependent upon selling not only your ability, but also your personality. Before an employer accepts you, he must not only be satisfied that your lettering meets his requirements, but he must also be favorably impressed by your general character. From the moment you step up to be interviewed and to show off your samples, he begins to appraise you mentally. The odds are certainly against you if his mental summation represents a shuffling lout who heaved a disheveled bundle on top of his desk inkwell, and tried his patience by fumbling with a knot meant for Houdini's magic fingers.

Your care in presenting the samples for consideration should serve as a mirror or index of the care you mean to show in doing your work if hired. You should look and act alive, and ready to "do things" without first having to be roused. Do not ruin your chances by insisting that your interviewer see every sample in your bag of tricks. Dramatize your presentation so that the fine points of the plates are highlighted, and regulate your pace by the tempo of his personality.

Even if the interview does not bring immediate placement, give some thought to the lasting impression you leave behind you. At your first opportunity, send a sincere letter of thanks to the person who interviewed you. Such a letter will serve you in two ways. First, it will label the communicant as a courteous person, appreciative of the important business time spent in consulting with him. Also, it will act as a memorandum of the sender's name, address, and special abilities. Whenever possible, this "follow-up" letter should be written on personal stationery, and it should in some way identify the lettering artist with the samples he showed at the interview. Then, when work of such a nature arises, he has a fairly good chance of being remembered and called upon to fulfill the assignment.

You will find that it costs no more to be courteous, neat, and considerate. These personal traits, coupled with high-caliber craftsmanship, diffuse an optimistic glow on the future of one seeking to make a name for himself in the world of lettering.

Bibliography

Berger, Richard — BROCHURE OF CONTEMPORARY ALPHABETS
Georgian House   1936

Biegeleisen, J. I. — SILK SCREEN STENCIL CRAFT AS A HOBBY
Harper & Brothers   1939

Biegeleisen, J. I., and Busenbark, E. J. — SILK SCREEN PRINTING PROCESS
McGraw-Hill Book Company   1938

Blair, Lawrence E. — PRINCIPLES AND PRACTICE OF SHOW-CARD WRITING
McGraw-Hill Book Company   1937

Carlyle, Paul, and Oring, Guy — LETTERS AND LETTERING
McGraw-Hill Book Company   1938

Carlyle, Paul, and Oring, Guy — LEARNING TO LETTER
McGraw-Hill Book Company   1939

Chappell, Warren — THE ANATOMY OF LETTERING
Loring and Mussey   1935

Cooper, Austin — MAKING A POSTER
Studio Limited   1938

Day, Harold H. — MODERN BRUSH LETTERING
Signs of Times Publishing Company   1931

Dwiggins, W. A. — LAYOUT IN ADVERTISING
Harper & Brothers   1928

Evetts, L. C.   ROMAN LETTERING
                                     Pitman Publishing Company   1938

Gordon, William H.   LETTERING
                                     Signs of Times Publishing Company   1920

Goudy, Frederic W.   ELEMENTS OF LETTERING
                                     Mitchell Kennerley   1926

Goudy, Frederic W.   THE ALPHABET
                                     Mitchell Kennerley   1926

Heller, Maxwell L.   NEW STANDARD LETTERER AND SHOWCARD WRITER
                                     Library Press Limited   1926

Hewitt, Graily   LETTERING FOR STUDENTS AND CRAFTSMEN
                                     J. B. Lippincott Company   1930

Hunt, W. B., and Hunt, E. C.   FIFTY ALPHABETS
                                     Bruce Publishing Company   1931

Johnston, Edward   WRITING & ILLUMINATING & LETTERING
                                     Sir Isaac Pitman & Sons, Ltd.   1927

Lutz, E. G.   PRACTICAL ART LETTERING
                                     Charles Scribner's Sons   1930

Mitchel, F. J.   PRACTICAL LETTERING AND LAYOUT
                                     A. and C. Black, Ltd.   1935

Price, Matlack

LETTERING
Art Education, Inc.   1937

Ross, Frederick G.

MODERN LETTERING FOR PEN & BRUSH DESIGN
Hunt Pen Company   1938

Smith, Percy J.

LETTERING
Oxford University Press   1936

Tannahill, Sallie B.

P'S AND Q'S OF LETTERING
Doubleday, Page and Company   1932

Wade, Cecil

MODERN LETTERING FROM A TO Z
Sir Isaac Pitman & Sons, Ltd.   1937

LETTERING OF TODAY
The Studio, Ltd.   1937

STUDIO HANDBOOK
Frederick J. Drake & Company   1935

Index